Once Upon A Time

The Mad River Valley

Kevin and Sheila Southwick Eurich

Kevin Eurich

Take Me Back
Waitsfield, Vermont

Once Upon a Time
The Mad River Valley

Take Me Back, Inc
Waitsfield, Vermont

Cover photo: John L. Baird, the author's great grandfather, with his team of Morgan horses.

Photos courtesy the Author's Collection and Waitsfield Historical Society

Book design: RSBPress, Waitsfield, Vermont

ISBN 979-8-9895106-0-3

Contents

Beers Atlas of 1873

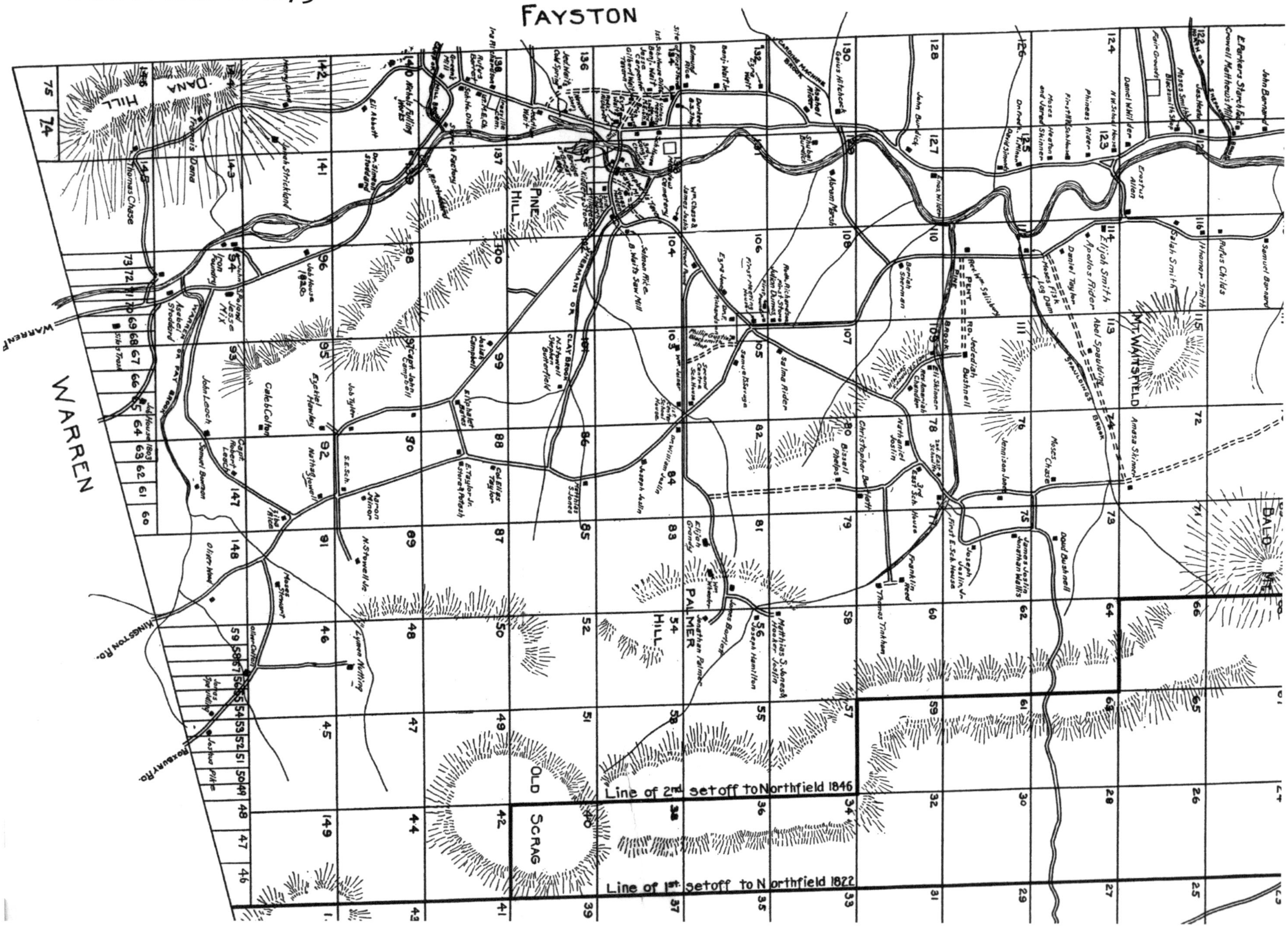

FAYSTON

DANA HILL

PINE HILL

CLAY BROOK

PALMER HILL

OLD SCRAG

WARREN

WARREN

KINGSTON RD.

ROXBURY RD.

MT. WAITSFIELD

BALD MT.

Line of 2nd set off to Northfield 1846

Line of 1st set off to Northfield 1822

About the Author

I am a fourth generation Vermonter on my paternal side and a sixth generation on my maternal side. I was born on April 19, 1947 at the former Heaton Hospital in Montpelier, VT. My dad, Clesson Eurich, woke up my grandparents, Earl and Etta Baird, to inform them that an additional farmer had been added to the family. I spent the bulk of my life in The Valley with the exception of living in Waterbury from 1957 through 1962 and my four-year hitch in the U.S. Navy (1965–1969). Graduating from Waitsfield High School in 1965 I enlisted in the United States Navy, serving until my discharge in Oct. of 1969. I served in Vietnam for about 11 months on the *USS Newman K. Perry* DD883, a destroyer keeled in 1945. My wife, Sheila (Southwick) Eurich, of Warren, and I married on October 20, 1968. Our daughter, Ginger, was born in June of 1969. In 1989, we were blessed with the birth of our grandson, Ryan Cubit, who now lives with his partner of ten years, Amanda Flanagan, and their daughter Cailin. The Navy provided me with training that was helpful in landing a job with Waitsfield–Fayston Telephone Company upon my discharge from the service in October, 1969. I retired from WFT in 2002 and did some writing for a couple of years or so and then went to work for Kingsbury Construction as a building and grounds maintenance person. In 2017, my wife, Sheila, and I decided to move permanently to Myrtle Beach, South Carolina where I started a handy man business. By 2019, I decided that I needed to do something a little less taxing and began part time work at Kroger's Grocery where I remain employed.

My family lineage is as follows:

Paternal

Great Grandfather, Heinrich "Henry" Eurich (1858–1951), was born in Fischborn, Hessen, Germany in 1858 and immigrated to the United States in 1878 (via Ellis Island) and responded to an ad by Henry Kew from South Fayston for a farm laborer which was common practice in those times. The Kew Farm was the last homestead at the end of the present day Tucker Hill Road. By 1889–1890 Henry's brother, Friedrich "Fred" Eurich had joined his brother and they purchased the Joe Tucker farm in Warren just over the hill from the Kew homestead. The exact location of the Tucker farm

Eurich Germany homestead

Heinrich and Sarah Eurich

Henry & Sarah Eurich with children

Clesson Eurich at
Mad River Glen

Mom and Dad at Highgate

Elwin and Myrtle
Sumner Richardson

Eurich, Blanche and Roy 50th
anniversary Warren Town hall

was behind the present day South Face Condos off the Sugarbush Access Road, just before the Sugarbush Inn. Henry married Sarah Long and they had three children; Roy, Dora and Lena. About 1940, the Eurich farm was sold and the family moved to their new home in Warren Village; first house on the right, Fuller Hill Road.

Grandfather, Roy Eurich, (1889–1963) married Blanche Richardson also of Warren. Roy and Blanche had six children; Marion (Neill), Edward, Clesson, twins Roger and Madeline (Kingsbury) and Christine (Crill).

Father, Clesson Eurich, (1918–1992) married Florence Baird (1920–2005) and they had six children: Nancy (Demas), Joanne (Griffith), Carol (Downer), Kevin, Susan (McDonald) and Steve.

Sarah Long (1866–1947) was the daughter of John (1821–1875) and Sarah "Baird" (????–1881) Long. John and Sarah emigrated from Ireland and spent most of their adult life near the end of Tucker Hill Road in South Fayston. John Long's brother was Robert Eastman Long and the author's connection to Robert's descendants.

Blanche Richardson (1892–1985) was the daughter of Elwyn "Ellie" (1869–1960) and Myrtle Sumner (1870–1959) Richardson. Elwyn and Myrtle married in 1881. Their home was located just across the small bridge at the bottom of West Hill in Warren.

Maternal

Great, Great, Great Grandfather, Patrick Moriarty, (1792–1890) was born in Adfert Parish, County Kerry, Ireland. He was married to one Nancy Crane, (died 1871) also from Ireland. Patrick immigrated to the U.S. in 1847 settling in Waitsfield, but removed to Northfield. They had several children, one of which was Michael.

Great, Great, Grandfather, Michael Moriarty, (1832–1915) was born in Ireland and came to the U.S. with his parents. After many years at sea, he settled in Waitsfield and built a home at the end of the present day Bowen Rd. In recent years, the land in this area was purchased by the Town of Waitsfield for public access. Hiking has become the most favorite past time there. The public parking lot is just about where the Moriarty/Bowen house once stood. The cellar hole can still be seen. Michael was married twice. His first wife was Jane McAvoy (1838–1878). They had several children, one of which was Anne Jane Moriarty. Michael's second wife was Johanna Ryan (1837–1904). They did not have children.

Great Grandmother, Anne Jane Moriarty, (1857–1934) married Albert Horace Bowen (1847–1935) in 1877. Albert was from the Bethel, VT area. Albert and Anne lived for many years in Bethel and eventually moved to the Moriarty homestead, remaining there until they retired to their daughter's (Marietta Bowen Baird) home on the Common Road. Being the last active residents there, the road was named after the Bowen family. Albert and Anne had several children, one of which was Marietta "Etta" Bowen.

Grandmother, Marietta Bowen, (1896–1979) married Earl W. Baird (1892–1976 in 1914. They lived most of their married lives on the Baird farm (owned by three generations of Bairds) which was located on the Common Road in Waitsfield, now the site of Ski Valley Acres. Earl and Etta moved to the village in 1964 after selling the farm. They had three children; Olive (Gile), Florence (Eurich) and Barbara (Eldredge).

Mother, Florence Baird, (1920–2005) married Clesson Eurich in 1938.

James Hugh Baird (1825–1913) and Nancy Baird (1826–1905 same last name, but not related) emigrated from Ireland and settled on the lot of Mathias Jones, an early settler of Waitsfield. This was the beginning of the Baird Farm. James and Nancy had several children, one of which was John L. Baird (1861–1935). John married Isabelle "Belle" McClarren Richardson in 1881. Belle's father was one John McClarren, but he gave her up for adoption. The reason was never known to me. However, they reunited in later years. Frederick Albert and Lorette Richardson adopted Belle. They lived "up east" somewhere in the area of what most know now as Toby Richards with reference to the Cutts and Ronks families who also lived there. John and Belle would have five sons, one of which was my grandfather, Earl Baird. When Earl sold the farm in 1964 the Baird farm era ended, although some neighbor farmers continued using the pasture land for cattle grazing and haying. By 1965, Ski Valley Acres was in full development.

Michael Moriarty c. 1890 single photo from collage

Jane McAoy Moriarty wife of Michael Moriarty, my great-great-grandparents

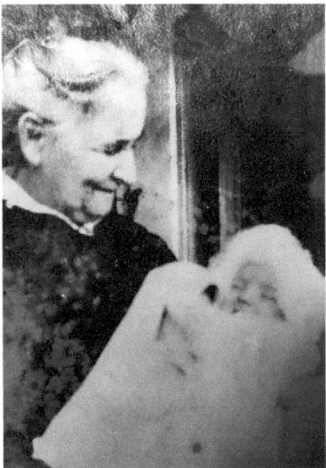
Anne Jane Moriarty Bowen and Olive Baird Gile

Marietta "Etta" Bowen Baird

Albert Bowen

Earl and Etta Baird 1961

The Baird farmhouse c. 1900. The area is now Ski Valley Acres on the Common Road in Waitsfield. The house was taken down around 2001, but the driveway and trees can still be seen. John L. Baird is sitting on the steps with his dog, Bonnie. Belle McClarren Richardson Baird standing.

Baird family: front row: Mark Baird, 2nd row left to right: Belle McClarren Richardson Baird, John McClarren, James Hugh Baird, John L. Baird. 3rd row: left to right: Clyde, Raymond, Paul and Earl Baird. c.1910

Florence Baird Eurich, Olive Baird Gile and Barbara Baird Eldredge

Earl and Etta Bairds daughters in front of the Baird farmhouse. Left to right: Olive Baird Gile, Florence Baird Eurich, Barbara Baird Eldredge. The 2 boys are cousins, Russell and Darwin Baird c. 1933

Introduction

I have an innate curiosity about history with emphasis on the so-called Mad River Valley or "The Valley" to most nowadays. I was blessed that both the maternal and paternal sides of my family had some avid photographers, "back in the day," which produced many photos that bring to life the generations that came before me. Couple this, with a father and mother and grandmother, Etta Bowen Baird, that shared memories from their past and I became hooked.

As a prime example, I used to hike up to the fire tower on Mount Alice behind Scragg Mountain. The way to the trailhead was via the Palmer Hill Road (ancestors of Everett Palmer and his son, Delbert Palmer) off the Common Road in Waitsfield and then a right turn that led to the original homestead of the Palmers. All that remained were cellar holes and sometimes rock foundations. There was even an abandoned well. I would stare at the old foundations and try to conjure up what this place once looked like and what the people went through living there. I've traveled throughout the Valley following old and sometimes ancient roads viewing what used to be homes and open land. I am a never ending bundle of curiosity; as if somehow the more I know will magically transport me to the time of whomever or whatever has my interest at any given moment.

Searches through antique shops for old photos and post cards rewarded me with some gems from the Valley's past. Time was another contributing factor as the family photo collections were handed down. And last was obtaining copies from glass negatives of photos taken throughout the Valley before and after 1900. Eleanor Farr Haskin of Waitsfield & Champlain Valley Telecom obtained the original glass negatives and had them made into slides. From there, they were scanned into computers for future reference and enjoyment. Because Eleanor's dream of museum never reached fruition, the photos ended up in the lap of the Waitsfield Historical Society (WHS). John "Jack" Smith and I went through these photos and identified about 80 percent of them for the WHS and now they are part of the Society's website. The late Jack Smith, of Waitsfield had the following lineage. His great grandfather, Patrick Smith, emigrated from Ireland. Patrick's son and Jack's grandfather, Josiah A. Smith, owned and operated a teamster business out of his home at 108 Bridge Street. Josiah was also a road commissioner. Josiah's son and Jack's dad, Herb, was a business man in Waitsfield. Herb's wife, Irene Labelle Smith, was Waitsfield's Postmaster when

Josiah, Herb, John Smith at 108 Bridge Street

Frank Lovette's barber shop Bridge Street

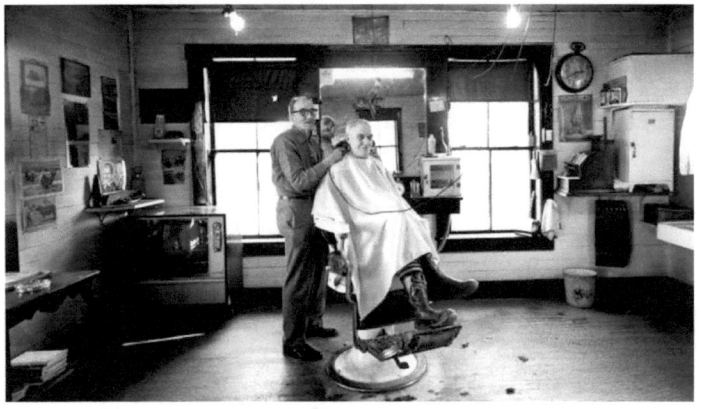

Frank-Lovett, barber and Harry Smith

the post office was housed in the Joslin Memorial Library, access being from the stairs on Bridge Street. Herb and Irene, during my time, lived directly across the street from the Smith house at 108 Bridge Street. They rented the Josiah Smith home for the income it could generate. While I was growing up and into my early adulthood, Frank and Grace Lovett resided at this home. Frank was a longtime barber with his shop located in the last building on the right before going through the covered bridge heading east. The building was torn down in recent years and a small park was built there. For my efforts with the historical society, I was given a DVD with about 700 hundred old photos. Not all of these are of the Mad River Valley and, as far as I know, Henry Cady (see Henry Cady in Section 1) took most of them. I have shown many of these on Facebook and therein generated the interest to a level that led me to put together this book of photos.

My most important message to the reader: I view this book as an ongoing work in progress. By that I mean to say I have written the narrative providing what I know. I am certainly not the end all to the history behind these photos. And, it is here that I will submit a disclaimer. I have made a significant effort to provide factual information. However a great deal of my narrative comes from information passed down through the years or what I have witnessed personally. This form of information transfer is always subject to embellishment and error. I do not profess to be a historical expert in any way, shape or form. This is a book of photos and the intent is for the reader to enjoy seeing the Valley as it once was and to stir memories. With that said, I would expect and strongly urge all readers to type up pages or make written notations of what they might know to add to the historical value and validity. Each of you will, in turn, someday hand your copy down to future generations. I see my project/my work as laying the foundation for all of you to build on. It has been such a joy putting this book together and I cannot tell you how exciting it is to know there will be many copies out there for people to get to know the Valley, "back in the day."

The opening section will include names of people from the Valley's past along with a short bio. These people surfaced during my research for the history of Waitsfield & Champlain Valley Telecom (100th anniversary in 2004) and their hand in how the Telco developed. However, these prominent citizens also helped build and shape the Valley in their own significant way. I will be entering their names with various photos throughout the book.

I would strongly recommend that the reader buy or somehow obtain a copy of the original *History of Waitsfield 1782–1908*, written by Matt Bushnell Jones as well as the subsequent *History of Waitsfield 1782–2000* book written by Richard "Dick" Bisbee. These historical documents provide a wealth of information up to 2000. The part that is of significant interest to me is the genealogy section from Matt Jones tome. I have used this data so many times in my research of Waitsfield. It will help pull some things together from Waitsfield's past. This would be the same for similar historical books or other such documents from the other towns. Further, I would encourage trips to the Town Clerks' Offices for additional information. It is where I spent a great deal of time researching my book, *The History of Waitsfield & Champlain Valley Telecom* (formerly Waitsfield & Fayston Telecom.) I visited so often that Rita Goss Kathan, Warren Town Clerk, used to say, "Kevin, who are you digging up today?" Much of the information I will provide in this book was gleaned from visits to not only town clerks offices, but historical societies and interviews with our elder generation still with us in 2002. I regret being 1,000 miles away from resources back in The Valley, while working on this project. I could verify a fact or garner additional information to perhaps stir a memory, but that wasn't possible.

I should add here that Mr. Cady's "community of interest" revolved around Waitsfield by-in-large. The consequence being that the majority of his photos are based in this area of the Valley. The paternal side of my ancestry is based in Warren and the maternal in Waitsfield. Given that, I hope it helps to balance things. Please enjoy the book; my labor of love!

Section 1
People of Interest in the Valley's Past

From 2002 through 2004 I worked extensively on Waitsfield & Champlain Valley Telecom's (WFT) history. This work was for the celebration of 100 years the Company had been in existence. The following people played various roles in Waitsfield-Fayston Telecom's (WFT) beginning and research provided me with what follows. However, though important to WFT, these people also helped shape the Valley's beginning and are important not only for what they did, but in providing history to some of the photos you will view:

Judge Jonathan Hammond Hastings was born in Waitsfield in 1824. His father followed the business of inn keeping, farming and the loaning of money. Being in ill health, Jonathan was called upon early to manage his father's financial affairs. His father died in 1857 and Jonathan ventured out into other businesses. For four years he was in a partnership with Richardson J. Gleason. Gleason and Hastings owned and operated a general store business in what is now the Masonic Lodge in Waitsfield. They sold the business and the building to Jacob Boyce in 1861. Jonathan was, by and large, a self-taught man and soon had the confidence and respect of the community. He was called upon to settle many estates as well as acting as guardian, trustee, referee, commissioner and business advisor. He was a director and vice-president of the National Bank of Waterbury. Judge Hastings also filled various town offices and was a deputy and later sheriff of Washington County. He was elected to the position of assistant judge for four years and served in the legislature, including a seat on the prestigious Ways and Means Committee.

Judge Jonathan Hammond Hastings

Richard J. Gleason was born in Warren in 1828 and attended schools in both Warren and Waitsfield. In 1849, he entered into employment with James McDonough Richardson of Waitsfield, remaining there for three years. His next employment was as a clerk for Cyrus Skinner. In 1856, he "conducted" a union store in the village (a general store located in the Larrow House) and later performed a mercantile partnership with Judge Jonathan Hastings, which continued for four years.

Francis "Frank" A. Boyce was born in Seabrook, NH in 1841 and educated in the public schools of Nashua, Boston and New York City. His father, Jacob Boyce, was a partner in a New York firm that manufactured furniture for the southern market, but the Civil War ruined that business. Jacob was a native of Waitsfield. In 1861, he returned to his early home and bought the business of Gleason & Hastings, which included the "Brick Store" (today the Masonic Lodge). Frank learned the business from his father and took over when Jacob died in 1878. He remained in that business until his own death in 1903, willing everything to his wife, Jennie (Ashley; her first husband was Franklin Greene) Boyce. Jennie's son, Charles J. Greene continued to run the business until the death of Jennie in 1918. As Jennie's administrator, Charles Greene sold the property to Walter E. Jones in 1919. Walter E. Jones sold the property to the Mad River Masonic Lodge on July 1, 1920.

Walter Alonzo Jones was born in Waitsfield in 1840. He spent his youth on his father Hiram's farm. According to *The History of Waitsfield* by Matt Jones, Hiram had farm land in both lots 114 and 123 which essentially takes in the Tucker (Bertha & Edmond "Tod") farm across Route 100 at the Meadow Road and much of the Elwin Neill farm land. Walter's primary education was received through the local public schools. His high school education was completed at the Barre Academy. In the fall of 1861, he entered the University of Vermont but had to leave during his sophomore year because of ill health. He graduated from Berkshire Medical College in Pittsfield, Massachusetts in 1865. Medical college was not the rigorous institution it is today. The requirements to become a doctor were not as stringent. Nonetheless, he received his medical degree and practiced his profession for a short time at Fabius, New York and afterwards in his native town of Waitsfield. In 1869, Dr. Jones, with others, bought a somewhat extensive mercantile business from his uncle (located in the second building on the right as one proceeds east on Bridge Street; Later to become Mehuron's I.G.A store, the yellow building). It eventually came into his hands only and he gave up his medical practice to pursue the mercantile exclusively. Dr. Jones was actively identified with town affairs, especially interesting himself in the educational progress. He, more than any other of his time, greatly improved the schools of Waitsfield to the extent that they were the envy of other towns. Walter A. Jones was a selectman, moderator often, and a side judge for Washington County. He culminated his many years of public service by being elected to the Senate in 1888. This was his last public office. As far as Waitsfield-Fayston Telco is concerned, his major accomplishment was bringing two sons into the world who would have a profound effect on its beginning and future growth. Dr. Jones' first son was named Matt Bushnell Jones, he being born in 1871. Matt Jones would become New England Telephone and Telegraph's Vice-President and convince one of his chief technicians to become involved with a little start-up telephone company in Waitsfield. That technician's name was Alton E. Farr, later to become father of Eleanor Farr Haskin, owner and President of Waitsfield & Champlain Valley Telecom. One of Matt's other important accomplishments was the writing of the original *History of Waitsfield 1782–1908*. Its genealogy section, alone, provides great historic value. Dr. Jones' second son,

Walter E. Jones, was born in 1874. He graduated from St. Johnsbury Academy in 1894 and took over his father's store business in 1895. Walter E. Jones would go on to become one of the corporate members listed in the 1904 Legislative Act that incorporated WFT. He would also become its first manager and keep an interest in its operation even after Alton Farr took over in 1908.

Alton E. Farr was born in Moretown, VT on November 8, 1881 to Lewis and Carrie E. (Miner) Farr becoming the 7th generation Vermonter. His parents divorced in 1887 and Alton went to live with his Aunt Abby Miner in Waitsfield and attended Waitsfield High School while his mother went to Massachusetts to look for work. In the fall of 1899, after taking a course with the American Correspondence School of Electrical Engineering, Alton entered the Construction Department of New England Telephone & Telegraph. Alton remained with NET&T's Construction Department until 1906. He then transferred to the Engineering Department, staying there until 1908. As it happened, Matt B. Jones, a Waitsfield native, had become Vice-President of NET&T. He knew Alton through the typical connections of small towns like those in The Valley. Matt still owned the home of his parents in Waitsfield (brick house next to the UCC Church) and spent summers there. Matt's brother, Walter E., was now the manager of Waitsfield-Fayston Telco (WFT). Walter strongly encouraged Matt to talk Alton into coming back to the Valley to take over operations of the fledgling telephone company. Alton jumped at the opportunity and embarked on his journey to take over the reins of WFT. Though the money was really no better, the family would be moving "up country" where a dollar stretched a little further. Alton made a deal with the current stock holders of WFT so he alone would own all stock. The offer stated that, for their stock, Alton would provide one year of telephone service, not to exceed $15.00. In addition, if by 1913 he wasn't providing good service, the stock would be returned to the original owners. The offer was approved by the following stockholders in 1908: Walter E. Jones, Z.H. McAllister, C.M. Richardson, C.J. Greene, J.D. Davis, J.A. Erwin, Richardson brothers (Meridan and Clarence), John S. McLaughlin, Fred Eaton, E.S. Joslin, O.G. Eaton, R.J. Browne, G.H. Hastings, M.J. Waterman, P.B. Gaylord, E.J. Long, Walter Moriarty, Charles M. Jones, R.J. McAllister, J. Palmer, O.H. Joslin, E.G. Sommerville, Josiah Smith, H.T.J. Howe, F.A. Bragg, C.E. Jones, F.F. Wilder, L.W. Seaver, S.J. Dana, O.J. McAllister, R.J. Gleason, V.C. Pierce, Harry Belden, M.L. Martin, J.B. Thompson, Stephen P. Joslin (Riford and Fletcher's father), L.H. Boyce, M.J. Robinson, Dan McLaughlin, George Wallis (Otis Wallis's father), S.C. Bonnette, C.H. Kew S.G. Mathews, John L. Baird (author's great grandfather), B.D. Bisbee, J.J. Kelty, D.A. Kneeland and Oscar Eaton. Alton contracted TB and died in 1940 leaving his widow, Eunice Buzzle Farr, holding the reins to the Company. Eunice, for all intents and purposes, ran the Company singlehandedly from 1940 until her daughter, Eleanor Farr, who had been raised in the business herself, had finished college and could take the load off Eunice. This would

Alton E. Farr

GAR building, Alton Farr on his 1910
Thiem with Clayton Demerritt

Eunice Buzzell Farr

Eunice Buzzel Farr
working outside

Eleanor Farr Haskin

Eleanor Farr
Haskin and her
father Alton Farr

be about the mid-1950s. Eleanor and her husband, Dana Haskin, took over the business in the mid-1950s, went dial in 1961 and continued to be avant-garde and forward-thinking owners of a very successful communications business, still owned by family.

Eunice Buzzell Farr (1897–1965) was a prominent citizen of Waitsfield although she kept a low profile. However, she took on a massive responsibility of running Waitsfield-Fayston Telco after the death of her husband, Alton Farr, in 1940. She handled every facet of the operation and it was common to see her out untangling lines and installing phones throughout the Valley. She couldn't afford full-time employees, but two men from Waitsfield helped out as time would allow. One was Joe Moriarty. Joe was married to Ruth Mann. Their daughter, Dolores "Dody" Moriarty would go on to a long career at WFTelco. Joe was an electrician by trade which came in handy for his telephony work. The second gentlemen, Gene Baird, uncle to Andy Baird, Jr. of the Baird Mill helped out much like Joe Moriarty. Eunice's daughter, Eleanor, along with her new husband, Dana Haskin, would begin helping Eunice run the Company and eventually take over in the latter 1950s.

Eleanor Farr Haskin (1931–2015) was born into the telephone business. She began as a young girl learning quickly at the feet of her mother, Eunice Buzzell Farr. Eleanor also eagerly tagged along with the men who assisted Eunice with the telephone company operation where her education continued. After graduating from college with a degree in music, she returned to the Valley to assist her mother with the operation of Waitsfield-Fayston Telco, eventually taking over completely in the latter 1950s. Eleanor was a natural as a business person and always looking forward Very innovated, she guided the small independent company through dial conversion and onto state of the art technology to bring her family operation to be a leader across the nation being the first in many fields, such as CATV, Long Distance Calling and Billing, Internet Service Provider and diverse networking. She also served on many national committees and became the first woman president of the Telephone Association of New England (TANE) and Operation and Preservation of Small Telephone Companies (OPASTCO). Her national committee work took her to Capitol Hill in Washington, D.C. rubbing elbows with U.S. Senators and Congressmen. Still, her simple and hometown roots never left her soul. She led WFT through the acquisition of GTE properties across New England and New York. Her piece of the pie was the telephone properties in the Champlain Valley region and WFT became Waitsfield & Champlain Valley Telecommunications increasing the customer base from 5000 lines to 25,000 with the stroke of a pen. Eleanor was a great leader and a wonderful employer keeping her employees interest first and foremost. Though her life was in more modern times, she was attached biologically and emotionally to the past of her father and mother.

Oscar G. and Orville M. Eaton (The Eaton Brothers) had a tinsmith business in the building on Bridge Street that later became the original location of Bisbee's Hardware (the blue building). Oscar bought out his brother's interest in 1888 and continued until 1894 when he sold the tinsmith business to Norton & Boyce (not the Jacob Boyce family). Photos of the so-called Norton Block will appear later in this book. After that, he put in a stock of groceries, glassware, stationery, flour and feed, with the latter as a business leader. He eventually added onto the store and began selling agricultural implements. His wide practical knowledge and experience with farm machinery made him a favorite with the local farmers. After the death of his first wife, Oscar married Addie (Miner) Bushnell. Addie was Alton E. Farr's aunt. Alton would later purchase Oscar and Addie's brick home, right, on the east side of the covered bridge. Eventually the back half of this house became the business office for Waitsfield-Fayton Telco and remained so until the mid-1960s when a new structure was built just north of Waitsfield village, diagonally across Route 100 from the Waitsfield Elementary School. Oscar Eaton's son was Fred Eaton (1878–1951). Fred married Emily Johnson (1881–1984, a centenarian). Fred and Emily lived in the second building on Bridge Street just after the Joslin Memorial Library. Emily was a long-time Town Clerk for Waitsfield.

Oscar Eaton

Clarence M. and Meridan L. Richardson were the sons of Ira Richardson. Ira was born in Waitsfield in 1816. He was one of Waitsfield's most stirring and representative men and intimately associated with its business and public interests. Most of his business ventures were located in the area of what is now known as Irasville (the unincorporated town named the area in honor of its prominent citizen). The businesses included a tannery, a general store, clapboard and custom sawing mills. The farm was located in the general vicinity of the present Mad River Green shopping center. Prior to the building of this complex, the farm was owned and operated by Howard and Walter Kenyon. The building located at 5222 Main Street was the original home of Ira Richardson. Between that building and the Roswell Richardson home (5274 Main Street) stood a structure that contained the original Richardson Store; gone for decades. The clapboard and custom saw mills were located just upstream from the present site of the Andrew Baird Mill, Route 17. Clarence and Meridan were partners and also tended to many interests of their father even after Ira's death in 1877.

Home of Oscar Eaton on Bridge Street, and later Alton and Eunice Farr, and their daughter Eleanor and her husband Dana Haskin.

Hugh Baird was grandfather to Fletcher (lawyer) and Riford Joslin (mill owner and operator and later produced wood products such as furniture out of his garage on Mill Hill in Waitsfield and later in Irasville). He owned what is now known as the Mad River Barn (2849 Mill Brook Road aka Route 17). Hugh sold the property in 1909 before moving to Waitsfield village. Hugh also owned and ran a mill across the road from his home on Route 17 powered by the hydro power of Mill Brook. His last residence was the large white house in the middle

Many owners of this building on Bridge Street. Savage, Griffith and Neill, Eaton Brothers and in more recent times Bisbee's Hardware

J.J. Kelty

Ziba McAllister of Waitsfield

of Mill Hill, Waitsfield. Fletcher and Riford both spent much of their youth at this location. Eventually Riford obtained this home and property, eventually selling it to Bob and Rita Joslin and then it was purchased by Betty Hyde, former owner of Mad Bush Chalet.

George Fletcher, of Moretown, was the original owner of a store across from the present day Moretown Elementary School. John W. Taylor purchased the store from Mr. Fletcher, calling the business Taylor's General Store. Eventually it would be owned by Merlin Ward (long time Moretown native) as an I.G.A. Store. A major fire destroyed the structure in the mid-1950s and the lot remains vacant.

Dr. E.W. Slayton, of Warren, operated a store in the building last owned by Albert Neill. Dr. Slayton ran his medical practice from a home on 275 Main Street although actually on Flat Iron Road in Warren. Much later this building would be the home of Ruth and Marsena "Shinny" Greenslit. The store building was located on a lot that is now a parking area for The Pitcher Inn. During its life the store was owned and operated by a Spalding. Harold Parker and Lawrence Ford (husband of legendary Emma Ford, long time Warren Town Clerk and active in town affairs) partnered in a store business there as well. The last to own the building and business was Albert Neill.

John (J.J.) Kelty operated a stage line in Waitsfield. He lived and operated his teamster business from his home at 4740 Main Street in Waitsfield. He also operated out of the former Fecteau building at 51 Dugway Road (Irasville). The stage, typically, transported passengers and goods between Waitsfield and Middlesex when an active train station depot was present there.

Henry B. Cady, photographer, was born in Roxbury and married Laura A. Sterling from Warren. Mr. Cady's legacy is the prodigious and accumulative photos he took, not only of locations around the Valley, but personal family photos as well. I still have old family photos with H.B. Cady's signature. I'm sure some of you readers do as well. Many of his photos are displayed in this book.

Ziba McAllister was born in Waitsfield in 1841. He spent many years as the Waitsfield Town Clerk and some years as Postmaster. Ziba was a community leader and served on many committees, including being president of Old Home Week in 1901. Ziba was a Civil War veteran. His residence was the site of Waitsfield-Fayston Telco's first switchboard. This house would later be the home of Floy and Harold Joslin and then King & King's Legal Office.

Section 2
Waitsfield

Masonic Hall Waitsfield. Downer restaurant in background.

The Masonic Hall in Waitsfield sits at the junction of Main and Bridge Streets. One of the oldest buildings in Waitsfield, it served mostly as some type of store until sold to the Masons in 1920. The original building, on this site, was built around 1830 and burned in 1845. The next structure was the one that exists today. Jacob Boyce purchased a store business from partners, Gleason and Hastings in 1861. Frank A. Boyce took over after the death of his father, Jacob, in 1878. Frank A. Boyce died in 1903 and willed the business, building and property to his wife, Jennie (Ashley/Greene) Boyce. Jennies' son, Charles J. Greene (note the C.J. Greene sign on the building), continued to run the business until Jennie's death in 1918. As Jennie Boyce's Administrator, Charles Greene sold the building and property to Walter E. Jones in 1919. This ended the buildings life commercially. Walter E. Jones sold the building and property to the Masonic Lodge on July 1, 1920. The building has changed little externally since this photo was taken around 1905. The restaurant photo was taken in the Village Square behind the Masonic Hall. The Downers owned and operated a restaurant and inn as can be seen by the signage. To the right is a partial view of a building once used by Henry Bettis as a barber shop. I remember, as a youngster, having Henry cut my hair. Both buildings were abandoned by the mid 1950s and razed.

Another angle looking at the Downer Restaurant. I do not know the woman on the left, but the one on the right is my grandmother, **Marietta "Etta" Bowen Baird** about 1910.

Downer Inn

Marietta "Etta" Bowen
Baird on the right

Lareau's from Pine Hill (known as Wu Ledges)

Waitsfield village looking west

Irasville with Waitsfield village in background. Taken from Dana Hill.

The Lareau Farm (now Flat Bread Pizza). This photo was taken from Pine Hill about 1900. The original road to Warren followed along the Mad River and through the covered bridge seen here to the left of the Lareau house. The buildings left center is where Warren and Mae Ketcham lived, moving there in the early fifties.

Waitsfield Village viewed looking west from Cassius "Cat" Joslin Hill. Much of the landscape was open at this time. The many farms in the Valley kept it so. The demise of subsistence farming saw the forest reclaim much of the land as we know it today. Prominent in this photo is the Waitsfield UCC Church as well as the perennial covered bridge sitting majestically across the Mad River. To the left one can see the Moriarty and Joslin Mills. The river is aptly named as we have seen throughout history, bringing many a destructive flood.

Irasville as seen from two different views. One is taken from Dana Hill and the other Pine Hill. The exposure from Dana Hill looking north provides a great amount of historical reference. The middle left show the original barns of the Ira Richardson farm. This is the present day location of the Mad River Shopping Center. In the foreground one can view the road to Warren as it was then. Lower left is present day Route 17. The Warren Road then followed as seen here (later in 1950 the intersection of 17 & 100 changed and the 100 was moved closer to Mill Brook). Lower right you can partially see the covered bridge that spanned Mill Brook.

The second photo was taken from Pine Hill looking west and provides another angle of Irasville. This photo was taken after the one above. The original Richardson barns are gone and a different structure in their place. This is the same barn that was later used by Walter Kenyon and his son Howard Kenyon. Bragg Hill is in the background.

Irasville from Pine Hill

The following is the **Straw/Folsom homestead** located south of Waitsfield on Route 100 across from the Bundy Road. Pat Folsom, granddaughter of Charles and Mae Boyce Folsom, provided some of the following information. Charles and Mae were married on Dec. 25, 1907. There is thought that a family by the name of Poland may have lived there prior to Charles and Mae moving there in 1908. The Folsoms had cows and chickens, making and selling their homemade butter and eggs in the community. Pat recalls using the churn as a youngster. Charles fell off a load of hay sometime in the 1940s or 1950s and broke his neck. Though he survived, his capacity for working was diminished greatly. He died in 1963. A few years later Charles and Mae's daughter, Pauline Folsom Straw's, husband (Buck) died and Pauline moved in with her mother. Mae passed in 1979. Pauline's brother Wendell "Ike" Folsom did as much as he could, keeping the homestead together, but taxes and upkeep became too costly and he sold the place around 1990. Prior to that sale, Ike had sold some of the farm's property. One piece was sold to John Macone who built and founded the Alpen Inn now Yestermorrow. The other land was purchased by Tony and Betty Hyde and became Mad Bush Chalet. This photo, right, shows the aftermath of the Folsom Brook flood just below the Folsom home.

Previously I mentioned the **Kneeland farm**. Though all the buildings are gone, the foundations can still be observed. On the west side of the Mad River behind the Folsom lot was the access road to the Kneeland farm. Though no longer used, it can still be found and walked. This road connected to the Ferris Hill Road which became the Dana Hill Road forming a loop from Andy Baird's mill to today's Route 100. The author's grandparents, Roy and Blanche Richardson Eurich were employed on the Kneeland farm when they were first married. In the 1950s, Milford Long owned the lot though he did not live there. Milford's home was in Waitsfield village and later became the Village Grocery. Below is a last look at the Folsom house northern view.

Maybe the earliest photo since construction is obvious. Kneeland farm in the background.

Folsom and Straw homestead with washout in road to Warren

Charles and May Boyce Folsom

Folsom House

Kneeland homestead

Joslin-Barnard farm

Joslin farm house Common Road (second house on the left after the junction of Brook and Common Roads heading south) in Waitsfield. In the 1940s and 1950s, Robert "Bob" and Rita Joslin farmed here later selling out to Don and Jan Barnard about 1956. The Barnards continued with the dairy operation until about 1975, though they continued to reside there. Don became a Lister for the Town of Waitsfield. Jan worked for many years at Mehuron's Store in Irasville. In the latter 1980s, Don and Jan sold the property to Gib and Sue Geiger and built a new home just south still on the Common Road. Gib and Sue continue to use the land and buildings for agricultural purposes and tourism attractions. Bob and Rita Joslin had four children: Kenneth, Raymond, Robert "Bobby" and Jane Joslin Sprague. Don and Jan had five children: Steve, Tom, Ed, Pamela and Dianna.

The same Joslin home (below) as the photo on the left. Steve Joslin identified the following people left to right. All Joslins: Francis Caroline, Georgeanna, Oramel (Steve's great grandfather), Perry (Steve's great uncle lived in the house next door now Reisses), Emily Christine, Stephen Perry (Steve's grandfather), Julia Bailey (Steve's great grandmother).

Joslin home and family

These are photos taken in Waitsfield Village. The top photo with horse and buggy is on the south end. The building, to the left, was later the home of **Elden "Bud" and Stella (Fuller) Jones** situated below Waitsfield Telecom's dial office. The building in the background is now Darrad Computer Services.

Photo below was the home of **Walter A. Jones**. This beautiful brick structure still stands much as it looked when the photo was taken around 1900. Walter E. Jones later owned this house. The next house in the background once owned by Earl and Harriet Jones (see next photo).

This photo was taken across the street from the Walter A. Jones brick house beside the UCC Church. The identities of the children are not known, but thought to be daughters of Matt Jones. Circa 1890.

Photo below was later the home of **Earl and Harriet Jones**. Earl owned and operated a bottled propane gas business when I was a youngster. The people in the picture are unknown to me. Taken in the 1890s this home is now owned by Wren Flemer Compere.

Waitsfield's second Congregation Church was located on the top of Mill Hill. Note the outbuildings used for the wagons, sleighs and horses for those traveling to church services. The photo on the right below is another view of the second UCC Church and also Waitsfield village taken from the vantage point of Pine Hill.

Waitsfield's second and third Methodist Churches, left below, (second inset) with the interior shot of the third Methodist Church. Due to financial and membership issues the Methodist combined with the Congregationalists in the early 1900s and the third UCC church became the **Waitsfield Federated Church**. The old Methodist church became Waitsfield's Community Hall hosting town affairs and a basketball court for Waitsfield High School.

Waitsfield's third Congregation Church, left below, around 1900; the interior shown prior to renovation on the right below. My grandmother, Etta Baird, played organ and piano here for 55 years.

Waitsfield village looking east with East Warren Road in the background

Waitsfield village looking northeast. Old creamery center right, Loop Road left.

Waitsfield Village looking north

Waitsfield village center looking north. Village Grocery now in the building on the left. Walter Jones home right.

Waitsfield village looking south. Old Community Hall right, now a business.

Bridge Street looking west

The building on the right (4857 Main Street Waitsfield) has been used commercially since its beginning. Once owned by **Carl Long** and later by **Joe and Ruth Moriarty** (Joe had an appliance store and electrical business there and lived in the apartment upstairs).

The building in the photo on the left can be partially seen in the Carl Long building photo. It had many purposes. There were apartments, a barber shop, **Great Army of the Republic (GAR)**

Hall upstairs and Waitsfield-Fayston Telephone Company's switchboard. The building burned in 1944 as shown in the photos left. The telephone switchboard was relocated to the Enos Brothers' building just north of Carl Long's building.

Waitsfield's simple fire company was totally overwhelmed and not equipped so Waterbury and Montpelier Fire Departments were called in. The GAR building was a total loss, but the Long building was saved as shown right. In the photo bottom left Carl Long, slightly stooped walking between the firemen, is seen inspecting the aftermath. The lot has remained vacant with the exception of a small building just south, once used to house Waitsfield Fire Department's fire engine. After the 1944 fire, out of the obvious need, Nelson Patch and others founded the modern-day Waitsfield Fire Department.

The Village Square in Waitsfield. Left below: This photo depicts the times when horse and wagon were the main means of transportation. The building in the background has seen many a family within its walls. Henry Brothers lived there. His son, Enos, remained there with his wife, Gladys.

After the fire in the GAR building (February, 1944) just south of this home, Waitsfield-Fayston Telco moved their telephone switchboard into the front room of the building where it remained until the Telco went dial in 1961. After Mahlon and Florence Jamieson sold their farm on the Common Road in Waitsfield (selling to Werner Von Trapp), they moved into this home. Later, businesses populated the structure such as The Troll Shop and Universal Micro. Right is a photo of **Waitsfield-Faytson Telephone Company's** switchboard back in the magneto days or as many knew it; "ring down." Ramona "Mony" Shaw (daughter of Carlos Shaw), long-time operator, can be seen handling calls in the front room of the Brothers' building. Much of Waitsfield's activity took place in this general neighborhood during those

times. It was common for operators to see people driving or walking around the village. Many times when a caller asked to reach a certain party, Mony and others would say something like, "they're not home. I just saw them by Mehuron's." Further, emergency calls (fires mostly) were handled through the operators. Upon receiving a fire call the operators would plug into the various lines of the firemen and produce a distinctive series of rings to provide a specific alert. From there, the operator would provide the necessary information. In the days before radios and other special equipment, the operator would stand in the

Ramona Shaw at the switchboard

doorway and direct those firemen going by that missed the call, but heard the activation of the fire siren on top of the firehouse just two doors south of this location. There were many who worked for WFTelco as operators and I don't have a complete list, but here are some that I knew about: Mony Shaw, Gladys Brothers, Sally Wimble Tremblay, Bernadette Ferris, Elizabeth Long Munn, Elizabeth Moriarty, Floy Bettis Joslin, Edna Boyce, Flo Cota, Ruth Cota, Katy Jones, Gertrude Baird, Elizabeth Hough Bettis, Norm Neill, Eunice Buzzell Farr and Eleanor Farr Haskin.

Right are two more photos of the **Village Square**. One can see the section of town where most everything took place at the time. Bridge Street starts with the Waitsfield House, a room and board business then. Continuing east on Bridge Street two more prominent buildings where commerce flowed and the heartbeat of Waitsfield citizens could be felt (in my time Mehuron's I.G.A and Bisbee Hardware). There was shopping, visiting and gossiping, especially on a Saturday night. The US Postal Service (not in view) was across the street in the Joslin building.

Middle right is another angle of the Village Square. The Brothers building is on the left with the Downer Inn on the right. Straight ahead, right, is the so-called Newcomb house and left background sits the John L. Baird (author's great grandfather) house and a more familiar name; The Dana house (home of Chester and Hattie Martin Kingsbury Dana).

Below right, the Jones family outside their brick home on Main Street in Waitsfield. Matt Bushnell Jones is on the left and his brother, Walter E. Jones is on the right. Matt and Walter were the sons of Walter Alonzo Jones (original owner of the brick house. See Section 1). Matt Jones had a great influence in Waitsfield. The original *History of Waitsfield* was written by him. Matt was a vice president of operations for New England Telephone & Telegraph and had, within his employ, a young Alton Farr who he convinced to come back to Waitsfield and take the reins of Waitsfield-Fayston Telephone Company in 1908. C. Early 1900s.

Walter Alonzo Jones, 1840–1892 home (below), later occupied by his son, Walter E. Jones. This house remains about the same as when this photo was taken around 1900. It is located on Main Street in Waitsfield next to the UCC Church. It is now primarily an apartment dwelling.

Bridge Street looking SE towards Pine Hill

Bridge Street looking west

Great Eddy on the Mad River

Covered Bridges were the norm until the 1950s when road improvements became a priority, parallel with President Eisenhower's interstate road system initiative which was inspired by the major highway structure in Germany he had observed during WWII. Further, the old wooden bridges were becoming a constant liability on towns with maintenance costs and load limit issues. The idea behind covered bridges was multi-fold. First the deck was protected, but equally important it made the horses feel more secure, as if entering a barn. Fortunately, some of these historic wonders have been protected providing a pleasing reminder of our past

Photo below left is of the High Bridge, a good 30 feet over the brook from Waitsfield's Brook Road (Junction of Brook Road and "Cat" Joslin Hill Road). Vern Parker can be seen driving his wagon and horse through the bridge. Background would be the junction of Bridge Street and East Warren Road.

High Bridge Waitsfield

Meadow Road bridge, Route 100 in the background

The photo below right was taken across from the present day Turner farm just north of the North Fayston Road. At that time the large mill existed on the west side of what would become Route 100. In the photo sits another covered bridge spanning the Sheppard Brook coming out of North Fayston.

The photo next page top, was taken just south of the covered bridge on Bridge Street. A dam existed at that time with a channel being dug from the east side of the Mad River and under Bridge Street to provide hydro

Turner farm and covered bridge

power for the Joslin grist and Moriarty saw mills. Though the dam was removed many years ago, one can still find the channel leading to Bridge Street. The Waitsfield UCC church steeple stands tall in the background.

The next few pages contain photos of mills in Waitsfield which have disappeared as time, economics and technology saw their demise. One noted mill that stood on Bridge Street (east side of the covered bridge) was the **Joslin Grist Mill** owned and operated by the Joslin family (Stephen Perry and Riford Joslin) over two generations. Steve Dole Joslin, son of Riford Joslin and grandson of Stephen Perry Joslin, provided a detailed narrative of this area in the village. Eventually the Joslin grist mill was morphed into a lodging facility for skiers coming north to enjoy the Valley's slopes. Miramar Ski Club has been in existence since the latter 1950s and continues to this day. Also in the area and behind the Joslin mill was the **Moriarty Lumber Mill**, owned originally by Walter Moriarty (father of Paul Moriarty and his sister, Mary) son of Dan Moriarty who emigrated from Ireland. A large lumber mill once existed in Herb Smith's (son of Josiah Smith) meadow behind his home at 108 Bridge Street.

In Irasville, brothers **Clarence and Meridan Richardson** (sons of Ira Richardson in whose honor Irasville was named) owned and operated a lumber mill on Mill Brook, Route 17 across from the present day Baird Mill. The mill was partly powered by hydro from Mill Brook. Though the mill is long gone some of the other structures associated with this operation still stand in the lot that Andy Baird and his father before him (Andrew Baird Sr.) used for stockpiling logs. During the 1800s and well into the 1900s mills were populated

Bridge Street, Waitsfield: Men making firewood in front of the Poland house. Background left is the original Joslin Grist Mill. The building in the center was once used as a cabinet factory and later mill office. Background, top, is the house that later became the home of Riford and Betty Joslin, Mill Hill.

Former home (house just before The Miramar Ski Club on Bridge Street) of Walter Henry Moriarty, owner and operator of the saw mill behind the Joslin Grist Mill. In my time, this home was owned and occupied by Elmer (1906–1989) and Aurelia Mehuron, founder of Mehurons Store originally in the yellow building on Bridge Street.

Waitsfield dam next to Bridge Street

Lumber mill in the Smith meadow off from Bridge Street, Waitsfield. The south end of the Waitsfield village is in the background.

Poland house

Moriarty mill Waitsfield

throughout the Valley; far too many to be listed even if I could remember. My father, Clesson Eurich, passed this information to me, often while hunting or fishing. He would point out where a mill had once existed, always providing details either from firsthand experience or what had been told to him by others. It was a way a life, when things of need were produced locally. Transport of materials, particularly lumber, was a daunting task, thus giving some credence to the amount of mills populated throughout the communities.

In the neighborhood of the Joslin and Moriarty mills, sits a brick and wooden structure. Many of those of my era referred to it as the Poland House but its history goes much deeper than that. The following narrative has been graciously provided by Steve Joslin as referred to above:

Kidder/Poland/Joslin House by Steve Joslin. In 1820, George Kidder constructed a wooden building on the current site which was used as a store and Post Office (Waitsfield). Sometime in the 1830s a brick section was added as a dwelling. Lewis Holden owned the property in the 1840s and ran the store. Ziba Rice owned the house in the 1850s and operated a cabinet shop in a building across the street and just east of the grist mill (grist mill was where Miramar is now). Arthur Poland owned the house in the early 1900s, most probably up to the late 30s or early 1940. Riford Stephen Joslin (1910–1970) and Elizabeth "Betty" Dole Joslin, my parents, bought the property in early 1941 as their first home. They were married July 23, 1941. From the various estimates, bills and proposals still in existence, it is evident that Riford and Betty completely redid the entire interior including the plumbing, electrical and heating systems. There is the possibility from looking at photos of the house during the Poland's occupancy that these systems may have been lacking or at least minimal. My mom and dad had the door in the west end of the house removed and a fireplace installed in its place. Betty and Riford continued to live there until the summer of 1948 when they moved into Riford's mother's home in the middle of Mill Hill on the left after his mother, Lena Joslin, died. Soon after, in 1948, Howard and Martha Moody purchased the house from my parents. Howard had been hired as the first manager of Mad River Glen ski area in 1948. They left in 1952 and the house was again sold. My daughter, Cara Beth, is the granddaughter of Howard and Martha Moody. The tree line on the southeast side of the house marks where a canal existed. This was hand dug in 1829–1830 and channeled water from the cove created by the log dam (built in 1830 as was the grist mill) existing on the south side of the covered bridge. The water ran under Bridge Street to power the grist and Moriarty mills. The sluice that was built to channel water to the two mills is still visible under the Miramar building. The wrought iron railing at the end of the concrete box culvert can still be seen on the edge of the road across from the ski lodge. In the early 1920s, Stephen Perry Joslin (1885–1934), my grandfather, and his cousin Ervin Joslin purchased the existing grist mill located across the street from the Poland House. Starting in 1938, Riford operated and then owned the grist mill which burned in December of 1944 (another major fire took place at the GAR building and Carl Long Store early in 1944) completely destroying the grist mill and Moriarty's saw mill (Paul rebuilt the mill powered by gasoline engine). Riford rebuilt the mill as a grain feed store in 1945 and this building is now owned and occupied by the Miramar Ski Club. Riford also transported maple syrup and maple sugar from the local sugar makers to the Carey Maple Sugar Company in St. Johnsbury, now Maple Grove. He used his 10-wheel grain truck for transporting. Riford also bought and shipped syrup to commercial accounts. At one time, he supplied the Pontiac division of General Motors with maple syrup in metal cans which the company gave out as Christmas gifts. In the later years, Riford owned a woodworking shop where he produced customer wood products. Riford's first place of operation was in the garage in the middle of Mill Hill across from his home. Later, Riford and Betty moved to Irasville and he continued his specialty wood work there.

If one drives up by Waitsfield Common and continues up the East Road they will come to the junction of Flood Road which leads to the Ronk and Cutts Roads (this area often referred to as Toby Richards). I should add that there was once the Northfield Mountain Road in this area. The author's grandfather, Roy Henry Eurich, was born at the base of this mountain road. Though the road has long been thrown up, it is still good enough for a major snowmobile trail.

Back at the 90-degree turn at the junction of East and Flood Roads there was once a school house (**Up East School**). Remnants of the foundation may still be found. My grandfather, Earl W. Baird and his brother, Raymond, attended this school and can be seen in the class photo taken about 1907. Many schools of this type were populated throughout the Valley. It was mostly done this way to deal with the fact that traveling wasn't the ease of which we view it today; wagons, sleighs and walking being the only form of transportation. In time, these buildings would disappear as transportation and the centralizing of schools was introduced. Walter A. Jones, an active participant in town affairs, had an intense interest in education and was a major catalyst for the improvements in education during these times.

Proceeding north on Flood Road one would go by the farm in the photo below. The Warren Willis Damon family rented this facility back in the earlier 1900s. The photo in this document is of Malcolm and his father, Warren Willis Damon. Additionally, I've attached a circa 1942 photo of Robert "Bob" Bisbee, childhood friend of Malcolm Damon. Both joined the U.S. Army Air Corp. (forerunner to the U.S. Air Force) and became pilots of multi-engine planes. Malcolm returned to the Valley about 1964 and joined his old friend in a partnership at Bisbees Hardware (when Bisbees was located in the blue building on Bridge Street in Waitsfield) where Bob specialized in plumbing and tin smith creations. Malcolm was the electrician in this endeavor.

In the late 1800s and early 1900s, things looked differently around the Valley. One notices immediately that there was much more open land. The demise of the farms allowed the forest to reclaim the land and, thus, takes on a much different view.

Logs going to the mill Waitsfield

Raymond and Earl Baird at Up East school
Waitsfield, Alice M. Bushnell 1904
Note the X's over Earl and Raymond Baird

The area know as Toby Richards

Robert C. Bisbee, 1944

Malcolm Francis and his father Willis Damon

Left middle is a photo taken from the Baird farm (now Ski Valley Acres) on the Common Road in Waitsfield looking towards what is now the home of the Von Trapps. Note that the barns are both sides of the Common Road. If viewed carefully, one is able to view the steeple of the First Congregational Church on the Common. In the middle right of the photo, one can view the roof of the Skinner barn. The next building beyond the barn was the No. 3 School (bottom photo) where neighborhood children attended, including my grandfather, Earl W. Baird, and his four brothers: Very top is Clyde Baird. Third row boy standing alone with short pants is Ward Joslin, father of Donnie Joslin. Next to Ward left is Earl Baird To Earl's right second child is Mark Baird. Second Row left with hands behind his back is Raymond Baird. Front row second from left with head bowed is Paul Baird.

Below is a view from the Cross Road in Waitsfield looking towards the Baird farm; now Ski Valley Acres. This is perhaps the oldest photo I have of this area. The flat top of the Freeman house has yet to be built. The Skinner barn can be seen at the lower left. Scragg Mountain stands majestically in the background.

Baird farm looking north

Multi classes at the No. 3 school. Skinner barn in background

Another view from the Baird farm is provided to the right. In the photo, lower left is the building that I knew as the Freeman house. Center below is the Skinner farm. Moving right is the present day von Trapp farm. In my time, this particular farm was owned by Clarence Tucker and then Mahlon Jamieson. Mahlon sold to Werner von Trapp about 1955. It has remained in the von Trapp family to this day with agricultural diversity.

The house on the bottom right was the home of John and Belle Kingsbury during my early childhood. Before that it was the childhood home of Riford and Fletcher Joslin. Eventually it was bought by the McTigue sisters. This structure sits left on Bridge Street just west of the covered bridge. John was a blacksmith; the shop sat on the east side.

Baird farm looking at Skinners, Freemans and Von Trapps

Larrow House, Waitsfield

Waitsfield band at the MIlford Long house

Jamieson, now von Trapp home

Photo above left: The building in the foreground was once owned by Richard Gleason and included a store on the ground floor. The Gleason sign can be seen on the porch roof. We, today, know this building as the Larrow house once owned and lived in by Everett "Jack" and Jessamine Bettis Larrow. In the background is the Methodist parsonage, now a private dwelling behind the Village Grocery.

The photo above right was taken in front of the former Milford Long residence; now the Village Grocery. Bands were a constant back in the day. This photo taken around 1895 is indicative of the brass bands that formed. Note the woman looking out the second story window at the photographer. Another photo on the next page of an organized band was taken in front of the former Carl Long store, later owned by Joe and Ruth Moriarty; now an antique shop.

John Kingsbury place Waitsfield

An organized band photo was taken in front of the former Carl Long store

The center of Waitsfield village was always the hubbub of the community. The photo at the bottom of the page shows the **Joslin Memorial Library** not long after it was built. One can also see the Masonic Hall, the Village Square and Bridge Street.

Prior to the Joslin Library being built, a bandstand stood in its place where many a concert was held. Also prior to the Joslin building was the so-called **Norton Block** (named after Jesse Norton who had a store there) which contained the original Odd Fellows Hall and a variety of businesses including a tin shop, the equipment of which ended up with the Bisbee Hardware Store. The Norton building's life was short as it burned in less than ten years after it was built under suspicious circumstances (1903). The two photos include the building (left) and the aftermath of the fire. Also in the photo is the band stand. Not long after the Norton Block burned construction began on the Joslin Memorial Library. A photo was taken of the work soon after it began.

Norton Block before the fire (above) and after (below)

Joslin Library under construction

Joslin Library completed

The author's great grandfather, John L. Baird, with his Morgan horses in front of the building that now houses Darrad Services (4457 Main Street)

1913 Ford The occupants are unknown to the author. The picture was taken on Farr Lane up from the Village Square in front of the Chester Dana building. The Joslin Memorial Library is in the background.

Baird boys behind the UCC church in Waitsfield. Top left is Clyde Baird, next to him is Raymond Baird, standing left is Earl Baird, next to Earl's left is Mark Baird and last, Paul Baird. c. 1906.

A drawing of the former home of Ziba McAllister later home to Floy and Harold Joslin (parents of Alberta Joslin Stafford). In more recent times it was the law office of King and King.

The second home of Herb and Irene Smith (first house on the left after the covered bridge) during my early time. Herb and Irene rented the original home of Patrick Smith and later his son, Josiah A. Smith, across the street. Eventually John "Jack" Smith returned to Waitsfield and took over the homestead of his great-grandfather and grandfather. Jack was married to Judy (Tucker) Smith. Judy was the daughter of Clarence and Charlotte Goodyear Tucker.

Once the home of photographer Henry Cady. Mr. Cady took many of the photos seen in this book and did personal and family photos all around the Valley. Most likely, longtime residents of the Valley have prints with the Cady logo on them. This house burned down. It was just before the former home of Bud and Stella (Fuller) Jones below the Waitsfield Telecom dial office. Note the Bell Telephone sign on the porch. This was one of the locations for public phones from NET&T.

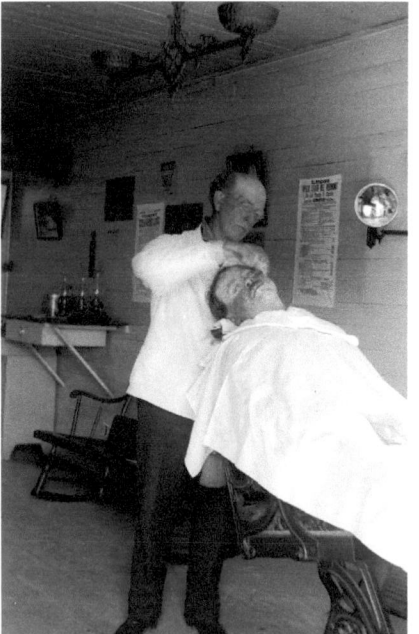

<Taken inside the barber shop located in the old GAR Hall next to the Carl Long Building. There is a sign on the wall dated 1909. It is unknown to the author who these people are. The GAR Hall housed apartments, businesses and the Waitsfield-Fayston Telecom switchboard until 1944 when the building burned to the ground.

The photo right was taken on Bridge Street in Waitsfield. Either this was a farm show or some cows got loose, but I'd go with the former. The bandstand and Masonic Hall can be seen in the background along with a partial view of the Larrow House.

Newcombe house above the Village Square built in 1845. The Methodist parsonage can also be seen to the right.

Bonnette's Garage c. 1940

All these photos were taken in the very early 1900s.

Above is Pearly Bonnette, founder of Bonnette's Garage. This photo, taken around 1940, shows the original building (a barn remodeled for the purpose of auto repair. It burned in the latter 1970s and was replaced by the basic structure seen presently housing the Mad River Valley Ambulance EMS service. Pearly's son, Harry Bonnette, took over from his father in the early 1950s. Pearly's daughter, Freda Bonnette Livingston, was one of the mechanics during WWII when most men were off involved in the war.

Alden Bettis, long-time Valleyite and WWII Navy Vet. Here he poses with his milk truck, co-owned by Earnest Chase. Alden Bettis grew up in the Valley and from early on was an entrepreneur. After the milk business, when televisions came into vogue, he had his own TV sales and service store beside his home in Waitsfield village. This building later became the Waitsfield USPS office and now is a wine shop. Alden created a public television viewing system long before cable TV was thought of by wiring the many homes in the village back to a common antenna point. For years after that system was abandoned one could find the original wiring strung throughout.

Norman "Norm" Neill (son of Harold and Harriet (Mann) Neil, their farm located above the Joslin round barn on the East Warren Road), another longtime citizen of Waitsfield. Norm worked for Waitsfield-Fayston Telephone Company in many positions, beginning his employment while still in high school at WHS. Here he is on a pole performing work on the lines associated with the old telephone system prior to 1961 before the Telco converted to dial service.

General Wait home

To the left is the original Waitsfield Elementary and High School built in 1847 (two-year high school in the beginning). In 1915, a large addition was built turning the facility into a full 12-grade school (the start of the 4-year high school). 1966 saw the last graduating class from this institution as towns joined forces creating union schools as a way to improve education possibilities and gain economies of scale. In the case of the Valley, that school was Harwood Union. After 1966, the old high school was used commercially for some years, but by the latter 1980s the structure was remodeled into condominiums and now is a full residential facility.

General Benjamin Wait
1737–1822

Above is the former home of **General Benjamin Wait** (1736–1822), original settler in the town named after him. A great deal of information can be obtained in Matt Jones' original *History of Waitsfield* regarding Waitsfield's founding father. Benjamin Wait's original home was a log cabin built on the Loop Road in Waitsfield, now known as the County Road. Later the log cabin was replaced by a single-story structure. The foundation for this house can still be found a short distant behind the former home of Eugene and Louise McNeil Moulton. The General died in 1822 and his original home was moved to the present site where a second story was added. General Wait was Waitsfield's first Selectman and the first church service was held in his barn.

The photo below was taken at the house just south of the old high school (4157 Main Street). In my time, it was the home of **John and Helen Fielder**. The big maple tree seen beyond the horse was still healthy and strong when I graduated from WHS in 1965. After the passing of both John and Helen, the building was purchased by Clear Water Canoe and became a retail store for outdoor sports equipment including kayaks and canoes.

The photo right shows the construction of the **Union Meeting House**, a non-denomination facility built to facilitate various town and other functions. This building was later remodeled and became what we knew in modern times as the Odd Fellows Hall. The Odd Fellows used the second story and the ground floor was an open floor plan with a stage on the west end of the building. Graduations, minstrel shows, proms, roller skating, movies and Memorial Day exercises were just a few of the functions that took place here. It is now the Valley Players Theater. The photo on the right shows the Odd Fellows Hall as it looks today. The eight-horse team shown here brought the Civil War Monument that was erected next to the Odd Fellows building.

The photo in on the bottom right was taken in 1910 at the **Odd Fellows Hall** (note stage in the background). This 1910 Waitsfield High School graduating class included the author's grandfather, Earl Baird (back row, right), and Earl's brother, Raymond Baird (first row left).

The photo above, during my early years, was the home and farm of Clarence and Charlotte Goodyear Tucker. Later this homestead was purchased by Stephen Flemer and is now owned by his daughter, Wrenn Flemer Compere. The big barn in the background burned before my time and was replaced by a new structure perpendicular to Main Street. To the left and out of sight would be the location of the old Odd Fellows Hall, now The Valley Players Theater.

Old Creamery

Dr. Carlos Shaw

Poland House

The top photo on this page is the old creamery which sat very close to the barn in the Tucker house photo on the previous page. The Loop Road (now County Road) is in the background. The creamery closed much before I was born in 1947 and I am told the building later had a variety of uses; basketball court, boxing matches and dances to name a few.

Dr. Carlos Shaw, middle left, on his rounds. This photo was taken on Bridge Street in front of the Waitsfield House. Behind the good doctor is the ground floor of the Waitsfield House. Many businesses were located here. In my time Walter and Agnes Kenyon operated a restaurant, later taken over by Joe and Ruth Moriarty. Later it became Seivwright Pharmacy. Doctor Shaw's home and office were at the former Congregational Parsonage on the east side of the covered bridge. This home can be seen in the background of the Poland House left below. The Shaw family came from the Roxbury area. One can travel on the Shaw Road on the Roxbury side of the mountain road.

Above is Waitsfield Town Clerk Ziba McAllister at his office. Ziba was the town clerk for many years and Post Master for a few. Ziba was very involved with town affairs and served as a Director of School Districts along with other involvements. There is speculation that this office may have been in his home, but I opine that it was more likely located in the GAR building that burned in 1944. The material used in this office matches that of the barbershop shown on page 23 which was located in the GAR structure. However, that is purely speculation.

John J. "JJ" Kelty Teamster Company (top right). JJ lived and operated his teamster business out of a building located at 4740 Main Street in Waitsfield. He also operated out of the former Fecteau building at 51 Dugway Road. He ran his stage between the Middlesex train depot and Waitsfield twice daily charging $.75 each way. Eleanor Farr Haskin found this same coach fully restored in Ohio through some massive research. She purchased it in anticipation of a museum which, sadly, never came to fruition. This photo was taken at the junction of the County Road and Main Street, Waitsfield. The Eugene Moulton home is in the background.

The house in the middle photo is located at 1184 Main Street, Waitsfield, south on Route 100 just after the Kingsbury Road. Clayton and Carolyn Joslin Kingsbury lived here in the latter 1950s and early 1960s. Prior to that, it was the home of Mervin and Madeline Eurich Kingsbury. Not much has changed since this photo was taken.

About a mile further south is the present-day turn leading to Butternut Hill. After crossing the Mad River the road turns sharply right and then a sweeping left. It is at this location that the Merritt Bragg farm once stood. In my early years it was home to and farmed by Robert "Bobby" Bragg, son of **Merritt and Hazel Bragg.** Sometime in the mid 1950s Bobby moved to East Montpelier. Katherine Bragg Johnson, daughter of Merritt and Hazel and a long time Valley resident, lived in a house on the left just before the farm with her husband, Merrill Johnson.

Kelty Teamster Company

1184 Main Street, Waitsfield

Left to right back row: Mervin "Mert" Kingsbury, Madeline Eurich Kingsbury, Dora Eurich, Roy Eurich, Blanche Richardson Eurich, Roger Eurich, Gilbert Thomas friend of the family. Bottom row left to right: Linda Neill Harvey, Roger Thomas Eurich, Sarah Long Eurich. Michael Kingsbury, Gary Kingsbury and Henry Eurich

Merritt and Hazel Bragg house

The Lamorder house on the south end of Waitsfield village. Mt. Ellen is in the background. The Couples Club field would be just beyond the tree line center. The author's father, Clesson Eurich, boarded here during the week while going to Waitsfield School.

The location is the second house south of MRVAS's barn. The building to the left was once the home to Palmer and Julie Gaylord. In the 1970s, an elderly gentleman, Bill Walters, lived here.

South end of Waitsfield village. The house on the right foreground is the same one as the house in the photo above. In the 1990s these were Ruth McGill's house on the left and Holly Meister's house on the right.

George and Hatty (Martin) Kingsbury, parents of Mervin, Clayton, Ernest, Elwin and George, Jr. George Sr. died young from lung disease brought on by his blacksmith profession. Hattie married Chester "Chet" Dana. They lived in the last house on Farr Lane.

The following photos were taken in Irasville.

Irasville heading into Waitsfield

Above the view is north with a prominence of the Richardson family in the foreground. The flat-roofed house and the three buildings on the left were all part of the Richardson family settlement. Ira lived in the third building on the left and, being a very involved citizen in the area with his hands in many businesses, Irasville was named in his honor. The last of the Richardson family that I recall from my earlier days was Maude Richardson who lived in the flat-roofed house, now the **Waitsfield Inn**. Meridan and Clarence Richardson, both sons of Ira, were involved in their father's affairs as well as developing their own businesses, including a grocery store and hardware store in the first two buildings on the left (the second one either burned or was torn down in subsequent years). The Richardson brothers also owned and operated a mill just up on Route 17 across from the present day Baird Mill. Agnes and Walt Kenyon would later purchase land and buildings in this area along with their son, Howard and his wife, Dorothy. Walt and Agnes continued the grocery business in the first building left and Howard ran the farm. That farm would later become the site of the Mad River Green Shopping Center. Mervin and Madeline Kingsbury along with Roger and Marion Eurich would purchase the Kenyon Store about 1959 and name their business the M&R Store, later building an addition and making it the first liquor store in the Valley.

Richardson Mill

The photo above right is also looking north, but shows more of the area, including the Kenyon barn as it was in my time. The Mad River Green Shopping Center tried to structure the new building to make it look like a barn which included a faux silo. Riford Joslin, after moving to Irasville, used the second building on the right for his wood working business, the Joslin home being the third building on the right.

Shown on the right bottom is the top end of the Brook road where it connects with the Common Road in Waitsfield. According to Richard Bisbee's *History of Waitsfield* book it was originally named the Wolf Road. When I lived on the Common Road next to the Baird farm

Skinner home on Cross Road

Everett Palmer barn on East Warren Road

Carroll Road

in the 50s, I often walked down this lane to the home of Joe and Ruth Moriarty to play with my friend, Richard "Dickie" Moriarty. This, of course, was prior to the Moriarty family's move to Waitsfield Village. Dickie lived on the Brook Road with his parents and siblings, Jack, Pat (Vanschaick), Elizabeth (Martin) and Dolores "Dody." This road was also a winter delight for long distance sledding. Roads weren't sanded as much as today and conditions often lent themselves to some breakneck speeds. Traffic was not a concern during these times, particularly in winter. I recall my grandfather, Earl Baird, teaching me to drive about 1959 and while driving on the Brook Road it was common procedure to honk the car horn as one entered the many blind turns on this road.

Above left is the photo of Harold and Alberta (Joslin) Stafford's home, during my earlier years. Later it would be purchased by Peter Boynton who converted the barn into a multi-purpose facility for theater and special celebrations. As most know, the barn is referred to as the Skinner Barn. The original home of a Doctor William Joslin (1780–1834), it was later owned by Henry Skinner (1827–1879) and then his son, Daniel Skinner.

Left is the Everett Palmer barn on the East Warren Road. Everett and Kathryn Palmer were very special to the people of the Valley. For over 50 years they produced maple syrup and maple products and ran a dairy farm. Everett was one of the bus drivers for the Waitsfield Elementary and High School during the 1950s. His route, as I remember, was the up Joslin Hill, East Road, Common Road and the East Warren Road. I rode on his bus when we lived on the Common Road next to the Baird Farm. A kind man, I later served with him on the Waitsfield Federated Church Board. Every year around Christmas time Everett and Kathryn placed a replica of Santa's sleigh and reindeer on their porch roof (a partial view of that roof is visible in the photo). It was the highlight of the Season for me coming from the Village on the way home.

Left is the westward view of the Carroll Road in Irasville. The homestead was once the home of Peter and Blanche Fecteau (grandparents of Bernadette Hood). They later sold to a Ray Thorpe. The barns have been gone for years, but the stately farmhouse remains. In later years businesses began popping up on the Carroll Road: Allen Lumber, Valley Rental, Edison Studio, Lawson's Finest, and the Big Picture restaurant to name a few.

The home, top right, housed or was owned by the following people: John Sloan, Levi French, Rueben Downer (ancestor of the author's brother-in-law, Phil "Pete" Downer), Paul Buzzell, Francis Bragg, Eben Boyce, Willis Bragg, Sewall Williams and Betsy Brothers.

Second right is a photo of the Elwin Neill Sr. (1915–2007) farmhouse, now owned by his son Elwin Neill Jr. This home is located on the North Road, just about ½ mile south of the Meadow Road in Waitsfield. Elwin and his wife, Florence, purchased this farm about 1942.

The bottom right photo on this page was taken in the Mill Hill Cemetery, Waitsfield. It was the dedication ceremony for the Revolutionary War memorial monument. This picture was taken in the very early 1900s. There must have been music as one can view at least two band members.

Below is a picture of the Wallis Homestead taken in the latter 1890s. This home was in the Wallis family since 1865. The Wallis family goes back to 1802 when Jonathan Wallis (1733–1818) moved to the area off the East Road in Waitsfield and started a farm. Jonathan's son, Joseph Wallis (1782–1860) took over after Jonathan's death. Joseph's son, Otis Wallis (1824–1893) purchased the old David Symonds' lots 124 and 125 in 1865 and this became the homestead shown in the photo. Otis's son George Wallis (1866–1908) followed in his father's footsteps. George's son, William Otis Wallis (1908–2003) took over the farm from George, farming until the latter 1960s before venturing into the insurance business and also sold recreation vehicles. William Otis left the property to his niece, Ann Wallis Bull, which she sold some years after W.O.'s death.

Sloan, French, Brothers home on Route 100

Elwin Neill farmhouse

Mill Hill Cemetery

MAIN ST., WARREN, VT, 15.

Section 3
Warren, Vermont

Main Street in Warren with a southern view. On the left is the Warren Community Hall back in time when a steeple graced the structure. It is still being used for special occasions and houses Warren's Historical Society with its vast collection of things past.

Left middle is another view of Warren's Main Street, taken in 1915. The first building on the left remained a store throughout its history. Dr. E.W. Slayton was most likely the original owner, followed by a man named Spalding. After that, partners Harold Parker and Lawrence Ford (Emma Ford's husband) operated here. The last business owner, in my recollection, was Albert Neill. It was an I.G.A store when Albert owned the business. Albert lived on the Flat Iron Road and made excellent maple syrup. The next building to the right would become the original Pitcher Inn. One can see the Warren Church in the background. Dr. Slayton practiced out of the former home of Marsena "Shinny" and Ruth Greenslit's home on Flat Iron Road the first house on the left from Main Street.

The photo below left is of the Orvis M. Jones Store just across from the Flat Iron Road. I believe it is now known as the Lippincott Building after one Carol Lippincott, former owner of the Warren Store. Note the Bell Telephone sign under the window. This was one of the locations for public phones coming from NET&T in Montpelier. When I was a youngster this building was dormant, but I used to look in the windows to observe pieces of equipment throughout.

The photo right is of Dr. Carlos Shaw making his rounds in Warren Village. He is walking from behind the Orvis Jones building where homes and apartments existed during those times. The Warren Church can be seen behind him. Dr. Shaw came from Roxbury and settled in Waitsfield. There is still a road on the Roxbury side of Warren Mountain named the Shaw Road where the good doctor grew up. He was father to Max Shaw, long time butcher for Mehurons Store. Dr. Shaw was noted and highly recognized for being able to make his own medicine, experimenting on himself before administering it to patients. He tended to the author's grandfather, Earl Baird, after he broke both legs in a fall off a

barn roof. There is no telling of the birth and deaths this man attended to in The Valley. He died around 1950.

Top right photo is Flat Iron Road in Warren. The Warren and Beverley (Graves) Mobus house is in the center background. The foundation for the barn is still very visible. The area where the Warren Elementary School is now was pasture land for this farm. To the left background is the former home of Norris "Fat" and Marlene (Neill) Weston. It's difficult to tell what is on the drays, but it would appear they may be heading for one of the many mills in the village.

The next photo below is of the Warren covered bridge. Without a doubt, it is probably the most photographed bridge in Vermont. At the time of the photo the Route 100 bypass did not exist and this one was the way to Lincoln Mountain. To go to Granville, one would go through Warren Village and then proceed south on what would become Route 100.

Two iconic structures in Warren are the old village school and the Warren Church in close proximity to each other. I believe the Warren Village School ceased existence in the latter 60s or early 1970 when a new school structure was erected on the present site of the Warren Recreation Field. The old school was subsequently reclaimed for the Warren Library and Town Clerk's office.

Warren village on Flat Iron Road, 1910

Warren covered bridge

Right is the junction of the Lincoln Mountain Road and Main Street with a northern view. The covered bridge would be left and just out of view.

Junction Lincoln Mountain Road and Main Street

Junction of Brook Road and Main Street

Left is the junction of Brook Road and Main Street. The building in the background was once a theater.

The photo in the middle is just south of the Flat Iron Road. Part of the Warren Church is visible on the right. This was prior to the latter 1940s when the Warren Fire House was erected. To the left is the flat-topped roof structure just beside the present day Warren USPS building. It once stood on the Flat Iron Road but was moved to its present location. The date of that move is unknown to the author.

The photo below left was taken around the same vicinity as above, but shows more of the area. The home on the immediate left was home to William "Bill" and Becky (Elliot) Peatman. The next house below that burned in one of the mill fires.

The third building is shown again below, was owned by Jesse Cota, long-time Warren native. Across the street one can view a little bit of the Town Hall and beyond that was the former Blair house, raised not too many years ago.

Jesse Cota house

Top right is a nice view taken at the junction of Flat Iron and Main Street. The house on the left was the former home of Marsena "Shinny" and Ruth Greenslit. Note the old street lamp on the second pole right.

Middle right is a view from the Warren Cemetery looking towards the Mobus home and what would become the Warren Recreation Field and the location of the new Warren school.

Below is a view from West Hill looking at Warren Village and Fuller Hill in the background. Open land was common for the times with so many subsistence farms scattered throughout the Valley, sheep farming being ahead of the dairy farming to come. Remnants of stone walls and fences can still be found for those who choose to venture a cross-country trip.

Flat Iron and Main Street

Warren Cemetery

Logging, of course, was another major activity with mills scattered throughout the Valley. And the various mills weren't just your traditional saw mills, but those that made specialty products such as clapboards, boxes for butter (the latter being at the bottom of West Hill behind my great grandparents' home (Ellie and Myrtle Richardson). The old dam just north of the covered bridge was built to provide hydro power for a mill that once stood in the same location. Mills were a major source of employment in times past, Vermont was truly an agricultural state then with conservative values, thus the promotion of the reticent Vermonter. Logs were transported to and from Granville and Hancock by way of a steam driven behemoth name Dinah. Right is the old relic sojourning through Granville Woods.

Snow removal or perhaps better said "snow maintenance" was accomplished not by plowing but by rolling with the hope of making a hard packed surface for horses, sleighs

Dinah the log hauler from Warren to
Granville two trips a day 1918

Snow Roller

In front of the Warren Store

and man afoot. Left is a photo of the author's grandfather, Roy Eurich and his cousin, Charles "Charlie" Patterson rolling snow in the about 1925. Charlie Patterson lived in the home of his parents, Sam and Jennie (Long) Patterson on the farm that would later become the Common Man Restaurant on the German Flats Road. This photo was taken on the Patterson farm.

The Warren Store was the hubbub of activity in the village. It became a natural location for gatherings to share gossip and maybe even do a little shopping. At the time of my youth and into the 1970s, the store was owned and operated by Roy Long, a distant cousin. Roy's son, Jerome, continued on with the operation for a few years after the death of this father. The middle photo left is a memorable photo including contemporary Warren citizens about 1960 in front of the Warren Store. In the front, row left to right: Merrill Long, Holly Greenslit with granddaughter, Vicki Greenslit Brooker and Clarence "Smithy" Smith. Back row left to right: Roy Long, Charles Ashley, Corliss, Roy Eurich, Frank Weston and Pearl Blair.

The Pitcher Inn (bottom left) today doesn't even come close to resembling the original, but it certainly dominates the center of the village across from the Warren Store. The parking area for the present day building is where the Slayton, Spalding, Parker and Ford and Neill store once stood.

The photos below were taken at the south entrance to Warren Village showing the home of Red and Gertrude Sutherland. The house and attached building still remain. Red and Gertrude's daughters, Judy Lisenby, now living in North Carolina and, Suzanne Austin, living in Moretown. The stone wall shown in the lower picture is still there.

Before it was a store, the building on the right was the Warren Inn. In this 1890s photo a prominent lawyer and orator, John Senter, from Montpelier, gave a speech from the Inn's front deck. He stands with his left arm touching his waist. Mr. Senter had the distinction of being in high demand for speaking engagements and argued cases in front of the Vermont and U.S. Supreme Courts.

The so-called Kingsbury Bridge spanning the Mad River had its beginning south of the site of the present bridge. It was an all wooden structure with the larger portion a covered version and the landing on the west side of the Mad River and open structure. One can still find the bridge abutment on the west side. The road swung left and came out where the Golden Lion Inn is at the base of the Sugarbush Access Road

Photo taken in the home of Roy and Blanche Eurich in Warren. The people in the photo all became part of the current "over 90 club." Left to Right: Carrie Lovett, Henry Eurich, Hod Elliott, Frank Blake and Ella Devall who lived to 105. Photo was taken in 1951.

South Fayston from Tucker Hill

Looking towards General Stark Mountain

Section 4
Fayston

Upper left, a view in South Fayston from Tucker Hill looking north onto Bragg Hill. The second photo is also from the Tucker Hill area looking west towards General Stark Mountain and what in 1948 would become the Mad River Glen Ski area along with a new road named Route 17 connecting the Valley to Bristol over what some still refer to as Mc-Cullough Turnpike. A.I. and Bessie McCullough lived in the house on the right just before the present day Fayston School on the German Flats Road.

Bottom left: C.D. Billings was one of the original incorporators and signers of the Legislative Act that incorporated Waitsfield-Fayston Telephone Company. His homestead would later be purchased by Sewall and Arthur Williams and converted into a lodging facility for the fledgling Mad River Glen skiing facility. The inn would be named the Ulla Lodge and later, in more recent years, The Hyde Away Inn and Restaurant located at 1428 Mill Brook Road (Route 17). This is how the Billings homestead looked at the time C.D. lived there around 1900. Note that there was a bridge crossing Mill Brook then for access to the Billings home. When Route 17 was built the road in this area was altered to what we now know. One can still see the abutment for this old wooden structure spanning the brook.

The photo left below was taken at the top of Number 9 Hill in South Fayston. The view is towards the west with Mount Ellen standing tall in the center. The house in the lower right would become the home of Guy Livingston in later years and now the home of his son, Pat. Tucker and Harris hill left and center. The photo below right was taken in Fayston 1914, but the exactly location is unknown. Though one wouldn't think so because of its size, this steam powered mill was considered portable and could be moved around the Valley as required.

Hyde Away on Route 17

Section 5
Moretown

I apologize for not having more photos of the Moretown area in my collection. As most know even today the name Ward was of major prominence in Moretown for over 100 years with Ward Lumber Company as a major employer and of much economic value to the little town. Here are three photos. The first two are of the taken at the upper and lower Ward Mills in the early 1900s.

The upper right photo is of Merlin Ward's I.G.A. store which burned in the 1950s. Originally the store was owned by George Fletcher. John W. Taylor purchased the store from Fletcher. During the time of Taylor's ownership in the early 1900s a public telephone was installed there, wired from NET&T in Montpelier. Since no other phones existed in the area for all intents and purposes the store became known as "telephone central" the town's connection to the outside world. Taylor sold the store to Merlin Ward

"Telephone Central" The IGA store in Moretown

Log truck entering the road down to the Mill

The Eurich farm in Warren as viewed from what would become the Sugarbush Access Road. The property was located up and behind present day South Face Condos.

The main barn on the Eurich farm. Note the bountiful garden foreground.

Section 6
Family and Friends Part 1

I dedicate this section to the many family photos from days of yore. Though many who read this probably wouldn't necessarily have an interest in my ancestry, I chose to include these photos with a narrative because it provides an historical perspective of the times.

As written in About the Author several people asked how I became me. I never knew Patrick Moriarty or his son, Michael or Michael's daughter, Anne Jane Moriarty Bowen. I never knew James Hugh Baird or his son John L. Baird These ancestors were always relegated to old photos. However, even though it is only snippets of foggy pictures in my mind, I do remember Heinrich "Henry" Eurich who died in 1951 when I was four years of age. In my mind's eye, the yellow suspenders and huge mustache are the physical attributes of memory for this man who emigrated from Germany in 1878 at the age of 20 and immersed himself in all things American including the English language. So dedicated to his new country, his grandchildren had to tease him to speak in his native tongue and then it was prayers only. Henry was painfully honest, walking miles to meet with a creditor to tell him face to face that he wouldn't be able to honor his debt on time. A kind mind, he was respected and loved.

During the times of my ancestry, life was completely different than what we know today with our fast pace, electronics and state of the art technology ruling our life. I believe more time was taken for the "act of living." The work was hard, but they knew when to rest and when to enjoy the respite from the rigorous requirements of the day. It is my hope that the reader sees both sides of life, "back in the day!"

The photo left middle is a closer view of the main barn on the Eurich farm. Below left to right: Sarah Long Eurich, Lena Eurich Richardson, Dora Eurich, Henry and Roy Eurich about 1900. The first picture on the following page is of Sarah and Henry about 1940 taken on the farm not long before the family moved to the village house on the Fuller Hill Road. This first house on the right just after entering Fuller Hill had been purchased earlier and used as rental income. At one point Frank and Grace Lovett rented there. Frank and his Waitsfield barbershop were shown in the Introduction

On the right is my Great Uncle Friedrich "Fred" Eurich, brother of Henry. Fred came to the U.S. about ten years after his brother and soon joined him on the farm in Warren, remaining there until

his death in 1935. This photo was taken on the porch of the Eurich farmhouse. Many in my family think my brother, Steve Eurich, has a very strong resemblance to his ancestor.

The photo middle right is of the Eurich family plus a long-time friend of the family, Oscar Neff a Swiss or Swede. See caption for identities. A special note about this photo taken in 1914: The baby in the photo, Marion Eurich Neill, would later become the mother of Morris Neill, Marla Neill Miller, Marlene Neill Weston and Linda Neill Harvey.

As discussed earlier there was always much to do on the farm and the following photos provide an example of the work. The Buzzells, Richard and Emily had a farm east of the Eurichs, but close enough to be within earshot. Richard and Emily were the parents of Eunice Buzzell Farr who would go on to owning and operating Waitsfield-Fayston Telephone Company. Eunice's daughter, Eleanor Farr Haskin, would later take the reins of the Telco and was the author's employer for 36 years. Eleanor shared that her grandparents would often hear the Eurichs singing as they worked in the fields. In the photo below right, Roy is on the load of hay while Gilbert "Gig" Thomas, friend of the family stands left. To his left is Henry Eurich. The young lad could be Ed or Clesson Eurich.

To say that hunting was a great pastime for the Eurichs would be a major understatement. Below is a perfect example of the group preparing for the hunt? I have to note that the two women on the right are my great aunts, Dora and Lena. These two were way ahead of the curve when it came to a woman's place in the world. This was around 1920 or a little before. That fact must be kept in mind.

Below middle is another shot of sisters, Dora and Lena on a hunt. Below right is a photo of the author's father, Clesson Eurich left (age 16), his brother Ed center and their father, Roy on the right; all bagging their bucks. Ed's was mammoth weighing in more than 200 pounds.

Heinrich and Sarah Eurich

Front row left to right: Blanche Richardson Eurich, the first Eurich grandchild Marion Eurich Neill, Roy Eurich, Lena Eurich, Oscar Neff and Sarah Long Eurich. Second row left to right is Henry and then his brother Fred Eurich

Logging in winter

Gig and Oscar on the Old farm

Clesson Eurich at age 3

Clesson Eurich with sister
Christine Eurich c. 1933

Left, logging in winter. Left to right: Henry Eurich, Ed Eurich, Gilbert Thomas, friend of the family, and Roy Eurich. If you owned a farm you produced most of what was needed. If lumber was a requirement you took your logs to the mill. The time it took for this load of logs was probably the entire day. In the background, is the sugar bush where the Eurichs made maple syrup by the barrel. After he stopped farming, Roy would continue with the sales and maintenance of maple operations equipment and then for the Town of Warren and Mad River Glen. The last photo to the left is of Gilbert Thomas and Oscar Neff (Swede or Swiss, not certain), both dear friends of the family. Gilbert was Welsh and became friends through Dora Eurich who became a nurse and worked at Marcy State Hospital in Rome, NY. Gil worked in the agricultural center.

The photo below right is of the author's father, Clesson Eurich (1918–1992), as an infant being held by his grandmother, Sarah Long Eurich, on the farm in Warren. The lower left photo is another picture of Clesson about the age of 3, taken on the Eurich farm. His favorite pet, a cat named "Sammy," sits in Clesson's cart. Bobcat Ridge stands in the background. Clesson was the third child born to Roy and Blanche Richardson Eurich. Below is a 1922 photo of the children. Their identifications are within the picture but incorrect. Swap Edward and Clesson. The last Eurich child wasn't born until some years later and it would be a girl, Christine. To the left below is Clesson holding his baby sister, Christine Eurich Crill.

Eurich Children - Circa 1922

Edward   Clesson   Madeline   Roger   Marion

The correct ID is from left to right: Clesson, Edward, Madeline Eurich Kingsbury, her twin brother, Roger and Marion Eurich Neill

Clesson Eurich with
Grandmother Sarah
Long Eurich

The United States entered WWII after a devastating attack on Pearl Harbor, Hawaii on December 7, 1941. Like most men who could, Clesson Eurich joined the Navy in 1944, serving until 1946 in the Pacific Theater. On the right is a photo of Clesson with a buddy prior to deployment.

Town team baseball was an important part of people's lives up until the latter 1960s and seems to have had resurgence of late. Not only did it provide for social networking and showing off one's athletic talents, it was also a great source of entertainment on Sunday afternoons, Memorial Day and July 4th. Clesson Eurich loved baseball and played a great deal in his younger life, including being a member of this 1946 Valley baseball team shortly after the end of WWII.

In several photos, I have listed people as friends of the Eurich family. My great aunt, Dora Eurich, was a nurse employed at the Marcy State Hospital in Rome, NY. There she met what became lifetime friends like Gilbert Thomas. We children called him Giggy. He was treated and respected as an uncle. The other person was Mable Pearce; she also a nurse. Though not related, she was fondly referred to as Aunt Mable. Dora made many a sojourn from New York to Warren to care for sick family members, a feat not easy at all in those times. It required a train trip to Rutland, VT and then a long car ride up secondary roads that were not good and very treacherous in winter! On the left, is a photo at the hospital in NY of Gilbert "Giggy" Thomas and Dora Eurich taken in the 1920s. Their trips back to the Eurich farm in Warren were often. It is Dora that we must thank for the myriad Eurich photos we enjoy today.

1946 Valley baseball team
Back row left to right: Cliff LaMorder (manager), Pat McCuin, Bob Bisbee, Clesson Eurich. Middle row left to right: Lyle Ford, Owen Ward, Guy Joslin, Bob Gallagher. Front row left to right: Lorne Whitworth, Willis Bragg, Clayton Kingsbury, Lawrence Kingsley. Front left is Jerome Long and his brother Sidney Long, right: sons of Roy Long.

Aunt Mabel, Aunt Marion, Uncle Ed and Clesson

Dora Eurich and Gilbert Thompson

Eurich farm access road with house in background

Dad's school class at the Down River School

Waitsfield High School Class of 1937
Waitsfield High School Class of 1937. Front row left to righ: Elizabeth Hough Bettis, Beverley Graves Mobus, Stella Fuller Jones, Albert Joslin Stafford, Edward Eaton, Norman C. Smith, Janice Joslin, Geneva Poland Howe, Florence Jones Jamieson Folson, ??. Back row left to right: Raymond Talbert Supt. Of Schools, Fred Armstrong, Malcolm Dana, Walter Jones, James Green, Clesson Eurich, Kendele Newcomb, Principal Donald Lindsley.

On the previous page is another dear friend of the family, Mable Pearce, known to all of us as Aunt Mable. Mable Pearce was also a nurse having met Dora during nursing school and they remained lifelong friends. In the photo on the Eurich farm she is holding the author's father, Clesson Eurich. To the left is Edward Eurich and right, Marion Eurich Neill. I am fortunate to have known Aunt Mable, Giggy and Aunt Dora well into my adulthood. A final photo provides a winter view looking at the Eurich farmhouse from their access road. The snow was shoveled by hand or some makeshift plow pulled by horses. My dad, Clesson Eurich, told me often about the walking trips to the Down River School, a building that still remains at the bottom of the Sugarbush Access Road, now a real estate office. The trip was about a three-mile walk one way and, contrary to lore it was up hill only one direction. Sometimes in winter the kids would use skis as a one-way means of transportation.

The photo left above is from classes that attended the Down River School at the base of the present Sugarbush Access Road and the junction of Route 100. The author apologizes for not having the names of all the students. Clesson Eurich is in the back row, the tallest. His sister, Madeline Eurich Kingsbury, is in the back row left. Madeline's twin brother, Roger, is in the back row right. It is thought, by the author, that the girl to Clesson's right is Margaret "Peg" O'Neill McCuin. There are also Defreests in the picture.

Clesson Eurich's WHS Class of 1937 left.

Earlier, I spoke of the eldest Eurich child, Marion Eurich Neill. Sadly, Aunt Marion died in her 30s after many years of bad health. But she birthed four children, three of whom are pictured here in this c. 1935 photo. Left to right, Marlene Neill Weston, Marla Neill Miller and partially obstructed Morris Neill. Morris was married to Jeanie (sp.) Shaw of Waitsfield. Not in the photo is the fourth and youngest, Linda Neill Harvey. After the loss of their mother, Linda was taken in by Grandmother Blanche Eurich and raised as her own.

Family and Friends Part 2

Thus ends the Eurich or paternal side of the author's family. Forward will be the maternal side including the Bairds, Bowens and Moriartys. Some of the photos have already been used in the About the Author section and won't be repeated here. That goes for the paternal family and friends previous.

Right is an undated photo of the Bowen, Moriarty home at the end of the Bowen Road in Waitsfield. Originally built by the author's great-great-grandfather, Michael Morarty, it later became the home of his daughter, Anne Jane Moriarty Bowen and her husband Albert Horace Bowen after they had lived in the Bethel area for some years where Albert was from. Their daughter and the author's future grandmother, Marietta "Etta" Bowen was in her later teens when the family moved here in the early 1900s.

On the right is a fun scene put on by Joe Regan left and Great Uncle Orville Bowen right. Watching the shenanigans is from left to right: Great Aunt Grace Bowen, Great Grandmother Anne Moriarty Bowen, Great Aunt Ellen "Nell" Moriarty Regan (wife of Joe) and Grandmother, Marietta "Etta" Bowen Baird

The photo on the left is of the author's great grandmother, Anne "Annie" Moriarty Bowen, right, with her sister Ellen "Nell" Moriarty Regan taken on the Regan farm in Bethel, Vermont.

Below is the birthplace of the author's grandmother, Marietta "Etta" Bowen Baird (1896–1979) in Bethel. This home is still standing. Included in this photo is, left to right: The author's great-great-grandfather, Orville Bowen (1810–1903), great uncle, Ted Bowen (1885–1945, sister to Etta) and great grandmother, Anne Moriarty Bowen (1857–1934).

Bowen Moriarty homestead

Aunt Nell and family with car Waitsfield

Baird farm from Cross Road

The photo left was taken from the Cross Road in Waitsfield looking SE at the site of the Baird farm. Scragg Mountain is in the background. In 1964 after the Baird farm was sold, this area was developed into what is now known as Ski Valley Acres. It is believed this photo is about 1875.

The small picture left is of the main Baird barn looking east towards Scragg Mountain. This building ran parallel to the Common Road. An attached barn, slightly smaller and unable to be seen in this photo, ran perpendicular to the Common Road. Note how the loose hay was stacked in small bundles throughout the field waiting to be pitched onto a wagon and then placed in the barn hay mows. Both barns were raised in the latter 1960s after development of Ski Valley Acres had been completed and the old farm house had been purchased.

Below left is a view looking west through the barnyard toward Mt Ellen. The other barn referenced above can be seen partially on the right. Note the hay wagon and the old mowing machine out and ready for use.

Below is the Baird farm house as it looked in the latter 1950s. Its appearance changed little until a fire in the 1990s and what was left was bulldozed into the ground around 2000. The large trees shown in this picture still stand and the driveway can still be viewed.

The top photo right is of the young Baird brothers c. 1905. From left to right: Raymond, Clyde, Mark, Earl and Paul. Raymond moved to New Hampshire and was involved in business. Clyde settled in Moretown and lived out his life there, working for as a Forester for the Vermont Agricultural Department. Mark settled in the Boston area where he was a director and teacher at an all-boys educational facility. Earl remained on the farm until his retirement in 1964 and Paul became a veterinarian, settling in Maine. The Baird men returned often for visits to the old Baird homestead where the author got to know them. All eventually married.

In the middle photo are the Baird women. This photo was taken, like so many, on the Baird farm, seemingly the nucleus of family gatherings and it remained so until it was no more. Left to right: Marietta "Etta" Bowen Baird, wife of Earl; Belle McClarren Richardson Baird, wife of John L. Baird; Bertha, wife of Paul Baird; Edith, wife of Raymond Baird; Zelta, wife of Mark Baird; and Irene Child, wife of Clyde. Irene worked in the Moretown Post Office when it was part of Ward's Store across from the Town Hall. Clyde and Irene lived out their married life in the building next to the so-called Chant building across from the library.

Below right are Etta and Earl in the courting days, not long before their marriage in 1914. This photo was taken on the Bowen/Moriarty homestead.

The photo left is of Earl Baird and his dog, Bonnie below the barns (a good view of both buildings as they were). Corn growing well in the background (c. 1925).

Earl Baird, Bertha Baird (Paul Baird's wife) and Clyde Baird at the Baird farm Waitsfield, c. 1920

Earl and Etta Baird Camel's Hump Club, c.1915

If you came to visit on the Baird farm you usually ended up working for your supper. Top left, Earl Baird sits on the wheel of the horse-drawn mower (later converted for a tractor pull). Paul Baird's wife, Bertha, sits in the operator's seat while Clyde Baird tends to the scythe to catch those areas the mower didn't get. There was no skipping over any blade of grass in those days.

Not everything was work for Earl and Etta. Left below is a group hiking Camel's Hump with a photo op at the Club House. Earl and Etta have check marks over their heads. Interestingly enough, there are other people from Waitsfield in the photo. To Earl's right is George and Hattie (Martin) Kingsbury and to George's right is his brother, John Kingsbury, and his wife Belle.

Above: John L. and Belle Richardson Baird at their son, Paul's, home in Maine about 1933. After retiring from the farm, John and Belle moved to the village and lived for a time in the last house on Farr Lane just before the Waitsfield Dial office. This later became the home of Hattie and Chester Dana. It is not known, by the author, whether or not the Baird's actually owned the building. Upon the death of her husband, Belle moved back on the farm with her son, Earl, and remained there until her own death in 1951. The author must note that, as he knew his great grandfather, Henry Eurich, in fuzzy mental photos, the same is applied to great grandmother Belle McClarren Richardson Baird A rather macabre but cute story from a four-year-old's perspective: When Belle passed her body lay in state in the Baird living room. This was common practice for the times and everyone would visit the home of the deceased to pay respects. The vivid memory I have of this time is my grandmother, Etta, and great aunt, Irene, trying on various specks (granny glasses) on Belle's face to see which one looked the best. In my mind, I only wondered why anyone would put glasses on someone who could no long see!?

Right: This photo was taken around 1933 on the Baird farm. Sitting is great grandmother, Anne "Annie" Moriarty Bowen. Standing by her is her granddaughter, Olive Baird Gile. Sitting second from left is Olive's sister, Florence Baird Eurich and last on the right is the third Baird girl, Barbara Baird Eldredge. The other children are cousins visiting the farm. The upper barn can be seen in the background.

Back in the earlier 1900s a fairground existed up behind the present day Our Lady of the Snows Catholic Church. The area has been used for pasture land by the Gaylords for many years. However, at about the age of 12 or 13 these three girls attended that annual exhibit. From left to right: Madeline Eurich Kingsbury, Florence Whitworth and Florence Baird Eurich. The year would have been about 1932. Note the wonderful cars of old.

The photo below was taken on the Common Road in Waitsfield just prior to the farm of Don Joslin. Hands on the reins of the trusty stead is Barbara Baird Eldredge, taught well by her father, Earl. Standing left on the dray is Caroline Joslin Kingsbury, daughter of Ward and Louisa Joslin. Next to Caroline is the author's mother, Florence Baird Eurich, with her ever present doll. It is not known who the other two children are, but it is a pretty sure bet they are siblings of Caroline's. c. 1930.

Baird, Florence sisters cousins and great grandmother Annie Bowen

Mom Eurich with Madeline Eurich Kingsbury left and Florence Whitworth center old fairgrounds Waitsfield c. 1933

Florence Baird Eurich with her parents on a picnic, c.1939

sisters Carol, Joanne and Nancy

The photo top left was taken around 1939. This was an obvious picnic somewhere near the Valley, but unknown to the author. From left to right: Marietta Bowen Baird, Barbara Baird Eldredge, Earl Baird, cousin Howard Bowen, Nancy Eurich Demas, Florence Baird Eurich and the Baird's beloved housekeeper from Ireland, Margaret "Maggie" Robertson. Maggie regaled us with stories from her homeland.

Below a favorite photo of the author's three older siblings on the Baird farm about 1945. Left to right: Carol Eurich Downer, Nancy Eurich Demas and Joanne Eurich Griffith. Sadly, Nancy and Joanne passed in 2010, but the memories continue on and we hold them dear! Upper barn stands in the background.

The Baird Farm was a place of wonderment for the grandchildren. It was the gathering point for all occasions, made special by two incredible people; Earl and Etta Baird, patriarch and matriarch. The memorable stairs were reserved always for the young grandchildren and this sitting was no different other than it became the last when the farm was sold in 1964 and Earl and Etta moved to their new home in the Village. Though we continued to gather there, it wasn't as often. The first cousins were older and beginning to move on with their lives. However, this moment in time captures the essence of family and being together like no other

place could provide. Those of us who knew it feel it, but find it so difficult to describe. Perhaps the only word I truly feel is "HOME!"

Left is a photo of the author, his siblings and mother.

Left to right: Kevin Eurich, Steven Eurich, Susan Eurich McDonald, Florence Baird Eurich, Carol Eurich Downer, Joanne Eurich Griffith and Nancy Eurich Demas. Taken around 2000 at Jays in the Mad River Green Shopping Center, Irasville.

Below is the photo of Earl and Etta Baird in the latter 1950s still on the Baird farm. Both were reaching retirement time and I think you can see tiredness in their beautiful faces. Farming, as was done by Earl Baird and others of his time, was finished. Regulations and costs were driving the subsistence farmer out of the business of family farming. Quietly, they sold the farm which was developed into residential real estate called Ski Valley Acres. This took place in 1963 and 1964. They had a house built in the Village off the Parsonage Road, behind the present day Village Grocery. Earl died in 1976 followed three years later by Etta in 1979. These two toiled to make ends meet and provide a future for their children. But they never lost their zest to somehow procure the magic of that old farm where we youngsters reveled in its luxury of mystery, fun and celebration. There will never be another like it. In our old age, we still live it and that is a sincere tribute to the two we lovingly knew as Nana and Grampa.

Baird farm porch

Earl and Etta Bowen Baird Common
Road Farm Waitsfield 1950s

Section 7
Notes, Stories, This & That

Alton Farr is written about earlier in the book, but I would be remiss for not providing more information on his many accomplishments and his relationship with The Valley and its citizens. I'm taking the following from my research for the *History of Waitsfield-Fayston Telephone Company*. It is rather full, but I will try to place it in line item for some expediency:

After graduating from Waitsfield High School at age 17, Alton returned to live with his mother, Carrie Lewis Miner, in the Boston area and attended a three-month business course at Gloucester Business College. He then attended the Mt. Herman School for Boys for a period of one year. Mt. Herman's curriculum was tough and designed for academic excellence. Successful completion put one in the status of having completed a freshman year in college. The tuition was $100.00 a year, a steep price for the times and since Carrie couldn't afford it, Alton dropped out. In the summer of 1899, Alton took employment as a bellhop on Campobello Island which is on the border of Maine and New Brunswick. Campobello was also the summer home of Franklin D. Roosevelt's family. In the fall of 1899, after taking a course with the American Correspondence School of Electrical Engineering, Alton entered the Construction Department of NET&T. As written earlier, by 1908, Alton had been convinced to return to Waitsfield and take of the Company.

After obtaining sole ownership of WFT, Alton moved on to building out the company's network, which until that time included only Waitsfield and south Fayston. He made deals with NET&T and eventually the network included Moretown, Waitsfield, Fayston and Warren.

It should be noted that during the early evolution of telephony the economies of scale dictated that it was only an affordable business for dense populations. This left the rural communities as the have-nots. Therefore, towns and individuals took it upon themselves to create networks, at least for the local use. At one time there was another telephone company operating in the Valley. It was out of Northfield, owned and operated by one, G.R.

Andrews. Andrews had stretched the network into Warren and down the East Warren Road to Waitsfield. Josiah Smith, a teamster in the Waitsfield Village took advantage of the two companies to expand his business and had a phone from each company installed in his house. Childhood neighbor, Mary Moriarty, recalled observing Josiah working both phones which fascinated her. G.R. was bought out by WFT in 1918.

WFT's telephone switchboard moved from time to time dependent on available space, rent and other logistics. By 1910, Alton knew he needed a more permanent location with space for his operators, including a bed to sleep on during the wee hours. He entered into rental deal with Earnest Chase (owner of the GAR building) for that purpose. Once the deal was signed the switchboard was moved from the Ziba McAllister residence to its new location where it remained until the great fire of 1944.

Speaking of which, Alton Farr was very involved in the then Waitsfield Fire Company. The equipment consisted of a handrail pumper and a chemical pumper, standard equipment for the day, but of little value for any major fire. Still having been traumatized by witnessing a fire in the First Methodist Church as a child, he was keen to try and protect his community. In 1910, Alton signed a deal for the WFC to rent a garage space on the south end of the old Waitsfield House. Carmi Gibbs was the owner at the time. The deal required Gibbs to pipe in hot air from the furnace to this room to keep the fluids from freezing in the fire apparatus.

Alton used all manner of vehicles to take care of the telephone company's requirements including two motorcycles. The first was a 1910 Theim and the next was a 1916 Excelsior. The use of motorcycles was common during these times.

Alton married Eunice Buzzell in 1923. Eunice was the daughter of Richard and Emily Buzzell. The Buzzells lived just east of the Eurich farm in Warren slightly downhill. This area is located off the present day Tishman Road. From all accounts, these two were special to the children in the Valley, especially in Waitsfield where they lived. Alton taught kids to swim and rigged a raft at the Great Eddy for diving and jumping. During the winter months he rigged lights up under the covered bridge for night skating. This was usually followed by hot chocolate and homemade potato chips made by Eunice.

Fletcher Joslin shared a story from these times. At the time, Fletcher was living in what would later become the John Kingsbury home just before entering the covered bridge from the west side left. He first met Alton when the latter used to come from time to time to change out the operating dry cell batteries in the phone. Wentworth Kew was a childhood friend of Fletcher's and Wentworth often borrowed his bike. The boy came up missing and Fletcher checked to see if the bike was gone which would have given an idea what he may have been up to, but the bike was where it should be. Wentworth was prone to go swimming by himself and fear so arose that he may have drowned. Alton knew the river well and if that were the case he had strong suspect where the boy's body might be found. Alton enlisted the help of Fletcher and they climbed into the canoe and found the boy exactly where Alton thought he would be. A tragedy and one that obviously never left Fletcher's memory.

Alton, through his training and his own devices, became an astute electrician and wired many homes in the Valley for this new luxury of power as it made its way into the rural communities making up the Valley towns.

Beekeeping, tree grafting and other forms of nature were the loves of Alton Farr. He owned land next to the Mill Hill Cemetery in Waitsfield. One can still find the apple orchard where he tended his fruits. He also kept the bee colonies in the area where they could work the fruit trees, flowers and other plants growing there. He once wrote an article for *The Vermonter*, the forerunner of *Vermont Life*, about how mother snakes take their off spring into their mouths for safe keeping during danger. He was taking issue with certain scientists that said it was a myth. Alton proved them wrong.

Though she was only nine when Alton died, Eleanor Farr Haskin remembered how well she was treated by him and the things they did together. Alton had a prickly side, but not when it came to children.

After the Flood of 1927, Alton single-handedly reestablished connection with the outside world by getting into his canoe with the necessary equipment and repaired poles and lines for 13 miles until he got to Middlesex where NET&T hooked him up to a Burlington line. His efforts made the *Barre Times*. Such was his dedication.

Telephony was still in its infancy and test equipment was, for all intents and purposes, nonexistent. Alton made his own drawing up schematics and then building the test sets with electrical parts and pieces, copywriting many of them.

There is so much more, but I think this says much about the man who helped develop the Valley communities.

Richard and Emily Buzzell parents of Eunice Buzzell Farr, Tishman Road

Clesson Eurich Warren Cubs town team baseball Valley, perhaps Warren Town team baseball c. 1935.

Front row left to right: Jimmy Hannon, Delbert Stearns, Ernest Tucker and "Red" Sutherland, score keeper. second Row left to right: Lawrence Ford, U. Sham (Lauren) Blake, Merritt "Bing" Jones, Ronson Tucker and Lyle Ford. Top row left to right: Clesson Eurich, Edwin Wakefield, Dennis Gove and Bernard Kew.

Waitsfield Federated Church youth group c. 1960.

Front row left to right: Wanda Gallagher, Helen Backus, Shirley Keith, Judy Jamieson, Paul Demas and Keith Moulton. Back row left to right: Peggy Folsom, Myrna Stafford, Karen Graves, Johnny Thompson; behind Johnny partially blocked is Kathy Gabaree, Edie Shaw, Greg Eurich, Becky Munn, Lynn "Jimsey" Bisbee, Priscilla Ketcham, Joyce Kenyon, Kristi Quackenbush and Brian Moulton.

Many stories came out of the days of the crank telephone and party lines. Following are a few I've heard about over the years.

Party lines were a luxury for bored housewives, I'm certain, but an irritant for those wishing to use the phone for a legitimate reason. One farmer kept picking up the receiver to see if the line was available only to hear two ladies talking about baking cookies. Finally, in exasperation, he sniffs loudly into the transmitter and says, "I smell something burning. You two ought to check your stove!" Click! Click!

Herb Dana's mother lived in the home just before the junction of Joslin Hill and Brook Roads in Waitsfield. She kept complaining to Alton about loud clicking on the phone when she used it to make a call. Alton could never find the problem when he tested. Finally he told her to make a call and the problem started immediately. At last, Alton notices that a terminal block's cap was missing at the feet of Mrs. Dana. It was during the days of metal hooped dresses and the fabric had worn enough for the metal hoop to make contact with the wires. Alton replaced the cap. Problem solved.

A.I. and Bessy McCollough lived on the farm just before the present day Fayston School on German Flats. It seemed that A.I. was going through an excessive amount of dry cells batteries in the phone at their home. Alton, after some sleuthing, determined A.I. was using the batteries to assist with a motorized appliance. Alton put a stop to that.

As referred to earlier, emergency (fire) calls were placed to the operator. The operator would in turn link the lines of the firemen and provide a coded ring. Then she/he would provide the necessary information. Radios and other electronics means of communications were not present in those days. But what they did have was a siren on top of the firehouse which, at that time, was two doors south of switchboard office. The operators would stand in the doorway to help flag down responders who heard the siren but didn't know the details. In this one event, Warren had called Waitsfield to assist with a barn fire in East Warren. Rounding the corner from Bridge Street and heading towards the firehouse was Eno Brothers and Willis Bragg. Now there is argument has to who said the following, but one of them hollered back at Gladys Brothers, "Tell them to keep it burning! We'll be there as soon as we can!"

Sugarbush Valley had begun around 1957. WFTelco still had the old telephone system and the newcomers were not favorably impressed with this backwards communications and often let people know about it, especially the poor operators of Waitsfield-Fayston Telecom. Mony Shaw was a consummate professional on the switchboard, but she also had a sharp tongue when she wanted to. She would answer politely and ask number please and such and would be greeted with disgruntled callers casting disparaging remarks and such. She'd continued with her pleasant approach and then would throw the key so she could not be heard and offer some expletives before returning the key to talk and continue on with her professional care. It was an hysterical sight to behold because she was so quick, one wondered if she'd ever screw it up. Not that we ever knew!

To the lower right is the former home of Robert "Rob" and Mayme Russ Livingston just west of the No. 9 School House on Route 17 South Fayston. Rob and his family also lived for many years up at the end of the Tucker Hill Road. Taken in 1902.

I have mentioned Bisbee's Hardware in this book and that it had its origination on Bridge Street in the Blue Building. It is here that I would like to add some detail. Clarence "Doc" Bisbee was born in Waitsfield, October 14, 1896 on the farm of his father, Burton Bisbee (b. Sept. 10, 1852) Burton settled the farm on Lots 103 and 105 which took up most of the real estate on the Cross Road between Joslin Hill and the Common Road. Doc married Dorothy May Savage in 1922 and had three sons; David, Richard and Robert "Bob." David was killed in action in the Battle of the Bulge during WWII. Richard Bisbee moved back to the Valley during his retirement years and rewrote the *History of Waitsfield 1789–2000*. Bob was a WWII pilot in either the B17 or B24, mostly as a state-side instructor. In 1944, Bob and his father, Clarence, purchased the Blue Building and at first operated a grocery store, but in a few years changed to hardware, plumbing and tin smith work, of which Bob was an expert. Malcolm Damon, lifelong friend of Bob Bisbee joined Bisbee Hardware about 1964 as an electrician and remained in the Valley until the 1980s. Malcolm grew up, "Up East" in the vicinity of the Toby Richards area off Flood Road. The Bisbees sold the store and business to Doug McKeckneay in 1972. When the Mad River Shopping Center was complete in 1974 Bisbee's Hardware moved there and remains at this location presently.

Mehuron's Store history goes back to 1940. Elmer Robert Mehuron (1906–1989) was the founder of Mehuron's. He married Aurelia Shaw in 1931. They lived on the east side of Bridge Street in the house of the left before the Miramar Ski Club. Aurelia was the daughter of Dr. Carlos Shaw. Elmer's original place of business began in the blue building on Bridge Street in 1940, but he moved next door in 1944 to the yellow building owned previously by Walter E. Jones. Aurelia and Elmer had three children: Alan, Anne Mehuron Dumas and Calvin. Alan (1931–1987) eventually took over the store from his father and sister, Anne worked there for many years after returning to the Valley. Mehuron's was an I.G.A. affiliate while established on Bridge Street, but went independent upon its move to the new shopping center in Irasville in the early 1970s. Alan was supported in the business by his wife, Irene, and later their son Tom would take over ownership and operation of the Mehuron's as he is presently.

It was important to me that I brought up some of the history of these two families and the services they provided during my youth and into adulthood. During the 40s, 50s and 60s Bridge Street was the nucleus of the town's heartbeat. Everything happened here. Progress

Robert and Mayme Livingston
Wedding photo
24 September 1903
Randolph, Vermont

photo copy courtesy
Stanley Livingston

Robert Rob and Mayme Russ Livingston

Robert and Mayme Livingston 1902
The house next to Number 9 school house

Eleazer Wells Tucker

Jeanette Palmer Tucker

John Long

Sarah Long Baird

forced moves for more space and bigger operations, but the memories of the small town stores and the personalities of the business owners and those who lived the life here will be a forever source of blissful memories.

I found photos of Clarence Tucker's grandparents after finishing the rough draft of this book. Trying to insert them in an earlier section proved a problem. I submit the here for your perusal. Eleazer Tucker (1815–1898) married Jeanette Palmer (1820–1898). Originally settling on Lot 60 (out beyond the old Earl and Richard Rivers farm), he removed to Fayston. Eleazer and Jeanette had a son, Alvaro born in 1863. Alvaro would become the father of Clarence Tucker (b. 1899). Left: Eleazer Tucker and his wife, Jeanette Palmer Tucker.

Earlier, I was listing my genealogy in About the Author section. I neglected to include the following two people who emigrated from Ireland and started the Long family connection in Fayston and Warren. Below left are John (1821–1875) and Sarah Baird Long (????–1881), parents of my great grandmother, Sarah Long Eurich who married Henry Eurich. They spent their lives on a farm at the end of Tucker Hill in South Fayston.

Below: 1959 Clesson Eurich bags a big one in Stetson Hollow, Warren and then brings it to the M&R Store in Irasville to show off to his brother-in-law, Mervin "Mert" Kingsbury and his brother, Roger Eurich. This was the original butcher area in the store that Mert and Roger had recently purchased from Walter and Agnes Kenyon.

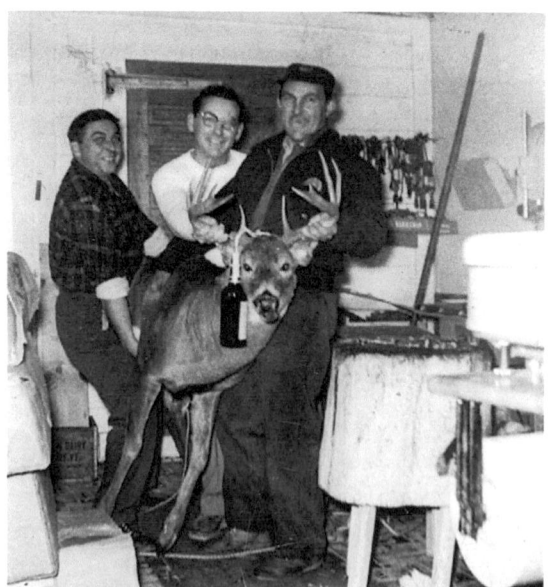

Mervin, Roger, Clesson and 10-point deer

Epilogue

An author always goes through the angst of wondering if he/she provided enough photos, enough narrative, but in the end it is what it is. My hope is that the reader has enjoyed looking back and remembering fond things from their own past in the Mad River Valley. Remember to add your own stories and notes to this book as it is a living document to be built on as I described in the introduction. I may be reached for comment on Facebook, E-mail (keurich@wcvt.com) or phone 802-223-4520.

Have a wonderful life and protect your memories and above all pass them on!!!